The Lava Tube

The Lava Tube

A Christian's Personal Journey with
Obsessive Compulsive Disorder

ROSEMARY BURKE

Foreword by Kevin Giles

RESOURCE *Publications* • Eugene, Oregon

THE LAVA TUBE
A Christian's Personal Journey with Obsessive Compulsive Disorder

Copyright © 2017 Rosemary Burke. All rights reserved. Except for brief quotations in critical publications or reviews, no part of this book may be reproduced in any manner without prior written permission from the publisher. Write: Permissions, Wipf and Stock Publishers, 199 W. 8th Ave., Suite 3, Eugene, OR 97401.

Resource Publications
An Imprint of Wipf and Stock Publishers
199 W. 8th Ave., Suite 3
Eugene, OR 97401

www.wipfandstock.com

PAPERBACK ISBN: 978-1-5326-1850-5
HARDCOVER ISBN: 978-1-4982-4412-1
EBOOK ISBN: 978-1-4982-4411-4

Manufactured in the U.S.A.   AUGUST 8, 2017

Contents

Permissions | *ix*
Medical Disclaimer | *xiii*
Foreword by Kevin Giles | *xv*
Preface | *xvii*
Acknowledgments | *xix*

1. Dread (My Acute Illness) | 1
    The build up
    The girl who felt unwell
    The tired-out boy
    The last straw
    Paparazzi
        Loose ends
        Unfamiliar territory

2. Disequilibrium (The Diagnosis) | 14
    What is this illness?
        The burned letters
    Statistics

Contents

    Obsessions and compulsions
        The word 'Obsession'
        The word 'Compulsion'
            The school bunny
        Scrupulosity—a common form of OCD
        My teenage years—evidence of early anxiety
        How is OCD diagnosed?
        How is OCD treated?

3. Darkness (Having Depression) | 31
    Not functioning
        Hold me Jesus
    Depression
        What I experienced
    Depression and the Christian
        The challenge of ignorance and judgement from critical Christians
    My cave analogy
        The Lava Tube
        My slipping and tripping recovery to health

4. Dearest (My Family's Experiences) | 51
    Mark
        Pathological doubt
    From my son's perspective
        His 11th birthday cake
    From my daughter's perspective
    'Law and Disorder'
    Helping the Carer
    In summary

5. Courage (Developing Treatment Strategies) | 64
    Cognitive Behavioral Therapy and Behavioral Therapy
        Obsessing and ruminating
        Distractions and rewards
    Prescription medication
        Challenges
            I'm knitting a Computer
    Anxiety management
        Keeping active
        Worry and stress management
        Biblical imagery—deep roots
            Courage trees
        Music and the sounds of nature
            Deep Peace
    Education
    Volunteering

6. Pearls (My Long Term Recovery Management) | 83
    Addressing my struggle with perfectionism and fear of failure
        Failure. When you're just not good enough!
        Risk
    Further CBT
        The Boxer
    Coming to a point of acceptance of my OCD long-term
    Put in place holistic strategies of self-care
        'Knowledge is power'
        'A precious flame'
        'Guard your heart for it is the wellspring of life'
        'Emerging inch by inch'

CONTENTS

    Recognizing triggers for anxiety
    Worms!
    The Inch Worm
    Rehabilitation back into the workforce and a new career direction

7. Determination (Recovery and Today) | 100
    Starting with a record
    The gold pen
    Setbacks and struggles
    The radio broadcast
    Finishing the marathon
    Today
    Volunteering and employment
    Feedback from family and friends
    My continuing hopes: the story of David and Goliath.

Appendix: Changing Tracks Broadcast, 10th October 2014 | *117*
Bibliography | *121*

Permissions

ARTICLES AND BOOKS

Anxiety Recovery Centre Victoria (ARCVic) Used with permission:
"Obsessive Compulsive Disorder OCD."http://arcvic.com.au/anxiety-disorders/obsessive-compulsive-disorder
"What is recovery?" http://www.arcvic.org.au/recovery/whatisrecovery
"CBT and Behavioural Therapy." http://www.arcvic.com.au/obsessive-compulsive-disorder/19

I'Anson, Kathryn. . . . *nine, ten, do it again: A Guide to Obsessive Compulsive Disorder For people with OCD and their families.* © Kathryn I'Anson-Dandenong: SmithKline Beecham, Obsessive Compulsive & Anxiety Disorders Foundation of Victoria Inc.

I'Anson, Kathryn and Carne, Rod, *A Guide for Young People with Obsessive Compulsive Disorder.* Ashwood: Anxiety Recovery Centre Victoria, 2005.

Better Health Channel, "Obsessive Compulsive disorder—family and friends." https://www.betterhealth.vic.gov.au/health/conditionsandtreatments/obsessive-compulsive-disorder-family-and-friends *This information has been provided by the Better Health Channel at* www.betterhealth.vic.gov.au

Deegan, Patricia. "'Recovering Our Sense of Value after Being Labelled Mentally Ill." *Journal of Psychological Nursing,* Vol 31 No 4 (1993) 7–11. Used with permission.

Dunjey, Lachlan. "Depression and the Christian," *Luke's Journal of Christian Medicine and Dentistry* Volume 7 No.3 (2002) 10–11. Used with permission.

Forty, Sandra. *M.C.Escher.* Surrey: TAJ INTERNATIONAL, 2009, M.C.Escher's "Ascending and Descending" ©2017 the M.C.Escher Company-The Netherlands. All rights reserved. www.mcescher.com Used with permission.

Krauth, Laurie. "Scrupulosity: Blackmailed by OCD in the name of God," http://lauriekrauth.weebly.com/scrupulosity-blackmailed-by-ocd-in-the-

Permissions

name-of-god.html used with permission. Also Reprinted from the OCF Newsletter Spring 2007. *Anxiety Matters* Vol 12, No 3 May (2008) 4,5,9. Krauth's article contains a quote from the following article; Nelson, J.S. Abramowitz, S.P. Whiteside & B.J. Deacon, "Scrupulosity in patients with obsessive–compulsive disorder: Relationship to clinical and cognitive phenomena", *Journal of Anxiety Disorders*, 2006, p 20, 1071–1086.

McGrath, Patrick B. (*The OCD Answerbook: Professional Answers to More than 250 Top Questions about Obsessive-Compulsive Disorder*). Copyright © 2007 by Patrick B McGrath Ph.D. Reprinted from the book The OCD Answer Book with permission of its publisher, Sourcebooks.

Parks Victoria, "Mount Eccles National Park—Visitor Guide and Walks." *Park Notes* March (2001) 1–4. Used with permission

Schwartz, Jeffrey M. *Brain Lock by Jeffrey M. Schwartz, M.D..* Copyright© 1996 by Jeffrey M.Schwartz, M.D. Reprinted by permission of HarperCollins Publishers.

Stokes, Jess. "Law and Disorder." *Warcry* Volume 121 No.7 (2002) 6–7. Used with permission

Yewers, Robert. "Psychiatry and Christianity". *Luke's Journal of Christian Medicine and Dentistry* Volume 7 No.3 (2002) 8–9. Used with permission.

Yount, Bill C., "I Saw Gold Pens Falling Out of Heaven onto the Earth." http://www.elijahlist.com/words/display_word.html?ID=1783 Used with permission.

LYRICS

THE BOXER (Sarah Groves) © Sarah Groves Music Licensed courtesy of CopyCare Pacific Pty Ltd. PO Box 314 Ourimbah NSW 2258

THE INCH WORM Words and Music by Frank Loesser © copyright Frank Music Corp administered by Kobalt Music Publishing Australia Pty Ltd. Print rights administered in Australia and New Zealand by Hal Leonard Australia Pty Ltd ABN 13 085 333 713 www.halleonard.com.au Used by Permission. All Rights Reserved. Unauthorised Reproduction is illegal.

HOLD ME JESUS written by Rich Mullins Copyright ©1993 Universal Music—Brentwood Benson Publ. Administered in Australasia by Crossroad Publishing.7 Broadway Street, Woolloongabba, Q. 4102. Email: copyright@crossroad.com.au Used with permission.

IMAGES

Figure 2: Rennert, Oliver and Australian Geographic—"Pipeline to History". Image extracted from article on Undara, a Volcanic Park in Queensland, courtesy of Australian Geographic. Used with permission.

PERMISSIONS

Figure 6: M.C.Escher's "Ascending and Descending" © 2017 The M.C. Escher Company—The Netherlands. All rights reserved. www.mcescher.com

Figure 10: Grimm, Michele and Tom. *"G3RRWC—A house cat with outstretched paws naps peacefully on its back on a soft carpet. He is exhausted, relaxed and sleeping as this close-up of his face reveals."* Alamy Stock Photo. Used with permission.

Figure 11: Cultura Creative (RF) *"E8AR39—Brown Bear cub playing (Ursus arctos) in Taiga Forest, Finland."* Alamy Stock Photo. Used with permission.

OTHER MATERIAL

Epstein, Rafael. Everything was obsessively doubted, and the life was all but squeezed out of me. "Rosemary-Changing Tracks." http://www.abc.net.au/local/audio/2014/10/10/4104443.htm used with permission.

Thomas, Lauren. "Anxiety and Depression" *Cultivate Training Session, Youth for Christ* 18/11/2009 used with permission.

BIBLE REFERENCES

NEW INTERNATIONAL VERSION (NIV)—for Scripture taken from The New International Version® Copyright © 1973, 1978, 1984 by International Bible Society.

The NIV Study Bible—for Scripture taken from the NIV Study Bible; Barker, Kenneth, general ed, Donald Burdick, John Stek, Walter Wessel and Ronald Youngblood, eds. *The NIV Study Bible, New International Version.* Grand Rapids: Zondervan. Scripture quotations marked (NIV) are taken from the Holy Bible, New International Version®, NIV®. Copyright © 1973, 1978, 1984, 2011 by Biblica, Inc.™ Used by permission of Zondervan. All rights reserved worldwide. www.zondervan.com The "NIV" and "New International Version" are trademarks registered in the United States Patent and Trademark Office by Biblica, Inc.™

NEW KING JAMES VERSION—for Scripture taken from the New King James Version®. Copyright © 1982 by Thomas Nelson. Used by permission. All rights reserved.

THE MESSAGE—Unless otherwise indicated, all Scripture quotations are taken from THE MESSAGE, copyright © 1993, 1994, 1995, 1996, 2000, 2001, 2002 by Eugene H. Peterson. Used by permission of NavPress. All rights reserved. Represented by Tyndale House Publishers, Inc. *Amplified Bible*

THE AMPLIFIED BIBLE—Scripture quotations taken from the Amplified® Bible (AMP), Copyright © 2015 by The Lockman Foundation. Used by permission. www.Lockman.org

Medical Disclaimer

THIS BOOK IS A memoir and is not intended to be used as a self-help book. It is also not intended to be a substitute for the medical and/or psychological advice of medical professionals. It is not meant to be used, nor should it be used, to diagnose or treat any medical condition. For diagnosis or treatment of any medical problem, please consult your own physician or a trained mental health professional. The information provided in this book is designed to provide helpful information on the subjects discussed. The publisher and author are not responsible for any specific health condition that may require medical supervision and are not liable for any damages or negative consequences from any treatment, action, application or preparation, to any person reading or following the information in it. References are provided for informational purposes only. Readers should be aware that the websites listed in this book may change.

My story may contain content that is confronting or distressing. If you need immediate or crisis help, please contact the free emergency 24-hour support organizations in your country, including

In Australia,
Lifeline Australia
Phone 13-11-14
www.lifeline.org.au

In the USA,
National Suicide Prevention Lifeline
Phone 1-800-273-8255
www.suicidepreventionlifeline.org

Foreword

I have known Rosemary for some years. For a time I was her pastor. In my relationship with her I always found her to be a very friendly Christian woman who usually had a bright smile on her face and was prayerful and keen to serve Christ. For a long time I knew nothing of her struggles with mental illness. I never suspected she had ongoing battles in this area. And I suspect few others did. Over time she shared with me on these matters and I was struck by her honesty and openness.

A couple of years ago she told me she had drafted out her story; a story about coping with depression, anxiety and obsessive compulsion disorder (OCD). She asked me would I read it. On doing so I thought this is a great little book; it will help lots of Christians who are perplexed as to why they have psychological issues when they are Christians. I also thought, Rosemary is just so open and writes so well this book must get an audience. I did note, however, that as a novice author Rosemary needed help structuring the book's flow for the reader. I offered to help her with editing and we worked on this for about three months. I learnt a lot about OCD and of how hard it is for Christians when they become mentally ill. They feel they have let God down and they sense others are judging them.

FOREWORD

Now Rosemary is ready to go to press. The story is 100% hers. I write this foreword to warmly and wholeheartedly commend her book. I think it is an excellent piece of work that will help many.

Kevin Giles
Pastor-theologian.

Preface

"You just need more faith, so that God will heal you."
    Hopefully, you find this statement as objectionable as I do. It is sometimes used by Christians pushing their agenda on someone else's situation. However, it is untrue and certainly not helpful to those suffering chronic illness.
    Views like this are even more painful and damaging to those with mental illness, because they reflect a profound misunderstanding of how mental illness affects the very core of a person.
    That single realization and my own experience of it became the trigger for me to write this book. Over the many years since then, God has prompted me in various ways to go further, weaving together my faith and my recovery. Obsessive Compulsive Disorder (OCD) and Depression are just as real in my life as my faith in God and his goodness, but it is my faith that defines who I am, not these diagnoses.
    However, this book is not primarily about faith or belief—it is about my journey of recovery from mental illness to a place of stability and fulfillment. If you are opening this book without a faith background, please don't stop here! Take this opportunity to look beyond any current fears, guilt or destructive thoughts you may have and discover the hope, joy and peace that can be recovered.

Preface

My purpose in writing this book has at its heart these three elements:

- To destigmatize this anxiety disorder in Christian circles. Christians do get mental illness; they are not immune. Anxiety is a real disorder and like many other illnesses, it can be treated. Statistics indicate around 2–3% of the Australian population suffer from OCD. It is not a "spiritual illness".
- To shed light on OCD in the hope that, by writing about it, an undiagnosed person with OCD might seek diagnosis and treatment much earlier that the average of three years.
- To encourage sufferers not to give up hope. God is still loving and almighty; Christian community fellowship is still real and beneficial to recovery.
- This book does not contain medical advice and I am not a medical professional. The information resources identified are intended to raise awareness about OCD so that the reader can make choices and take steps to seek professional help and/or manage their condition. This may include Christian spirituality and teaching, release from shame and active pursuit of a healthy and deepening Christian faith.

In taking the risk to expose my painful experiences, my hope and prayer is that this book will make a difference in the lives of those who read it, or their loved ones. May you discover the blessing of freedom from fear and guilt, recovery of healthy thinking, joy and fresh hope and faith for the future.

Acknowledgments

The Lava Tube has taken eight years to write. I had initially thought that it would take two years! But God knew better and I'm grateful to him for his precious patience and perspective on timing!

I have had such amazing support and generosity from so many sources in preparing my story. In particular I'd like to thank Ruth Pollard whose own story inspired me so much early after my OCD diagnosis. Also professionals Lauren Thomas, Patricia Deegan, Laurie Krauth and Rafael Epstein from ABC Radio Melbourne. I'm grateful to Oliver Rennert and Australian Geographic and Parks Victoria for their geological expertise in helping me explain the analogy of the lava tube and Jeanette for the gift of her poem many years ago.

Thank you to Lisa and my wonderful friends, whose encouragement always covered me with prayer and kept me persevering to see this book to its fruition. And to my treating medical professionals whose time and professional care made and makes all the difference to me, especially Dr Lal Fernando, Delmont Clinic, Melbourne Australia. Thank you so much to my ever-patient editors Jeanette Woods, Rev Dr Kevin Giles, Dr Denise Cooper-Clarke, Owen Salter, Leigh Hay and my husband Mark and all the team at Wipf and Stock Resource Publications.

Acknowledgments

Most of all I thank Mark and my beautiful family who lived daily with me through my illness and supported this project with endless encouragement. And a special thanks to my daughter for her delightful illustrations that bring special light and life to this book.

(For purposes of privacy, there are many names that I have not listed.)

1.

Dread (My Acute Illness)

THE BUILD UP

THIS WOULD BE A different story if I had tripped and broken my leg whilst walking back from our garden compost bin. If you break your leg, you usually get to choose the color of your plaster cast. Blue, pink or even purple, and there is much fussing and "oh silly you!" and flowers and casseroles. But no, my story is about how I broke my mind as I walked back from our compost bin, twenty meters from the back door. I didn't trip over anything, but something broke in me all the same. It was a crisp autumn morning. The sun was shining, the birds were singing, and I could not bring myself to go to work. It was May 26th, 2001. It was a momentous happening for me, but it had little impact on anyone outside my immediate family. I received a get-well card and letter from my workplace and then silence.

I 'broke' when I was forty years old, a wife of sixteen years and a mum of two small children. Now more than fifteen years later I am in my mid-fifties, with two young adult children. I was then and am now a committed Christian of evangelical and charismatic conviction. I firmly believe in God's amazing grace, his ability to heal and the power of prayer. This is my story of the psychological 'breakdown' caused by what is called Obsessive Compulsive

Disorder (OCD). It is also my story of recovery and how I learnt to manage it.

The first time I suspected that something was not right with my thinking was some nine months before my 'breakdown'. (On average, this period is about three years). After high school I trained as a nurse and worked with satisfaction in this field for over twenty years. When I became sick I was a part-time primary school nurse at my children's school. I had developed a pattern of worrying about all kinds of things and was finding it increasingly difficult to switch off and relax. I remember telling a friend that something wasn't quite right with me, but I couldn't put my finger on what it was. As a committed Christian I thought these long months of anxiety must be some kind of spiritual challenge that demanded I toughen up, face my fears and trust in God a lot more. Even though I really enjoyed coordinating the worship team at my church, I gave up this role. I thought reducing my commitments would solve the problem. Maybe then I would have more time to figure out what was going on in my head. In ignorance, I decided that these occasional obsessive worry loops were just one of the challenges of trying to balance family life, work, and church commitments that God wanted me to overcome by trusting him more.

THE GIRL WHO FELT UNWELL

Then one day at the school where I worked, a girl told her teacher that she felt a little unwell. She was brought to my sick bay. She didn't have a fever, headache, vomiting or diarrhea, rash, sore throat or three heads. After a twenty-minute rest she felt better. I wrote a note for her to give to her mum, as protocol demanded, and took her back to her class. Later her teacher mentioned to me, "I have just spent half an hour outside in the garden with Marylou.[1] She still feels unwell so I thought I'd give her some fresh air. She doesn't want to go home and she doesn't want to come back

---

1. Some names and identifying details have been changed to protect the privacy of individuals.

Dread (My Acute Illness)

to sick bay. I think she's okay to stay at school. The home bell will ring in half an hour."

Taken aback, I wondered why the teacher had spent time with her in the school grounds rather than sending her back to me at sick bay.

Suddenly I felt a 'click' in my mind and thought "Oh no! Did I miss something with her? Did I check everything? Did she not say she felt better? Should I have sent her home? What if she is seriously ill and I've missed the signs and symptoms and it'll be too late to save her"! Then the sensible Rosemary took over. I said to myself, "Don't be silly, you know she's fine. There's no need to worry."

That weekend we were booked as a family into a beautiful homestead snuggled in 'the bush'. It was a ministry retreat arranged by those working with my husband Mark. I knew I would not enjoy the weekend because I did not know what was happening to the girl I had seen the day before. Questions kept flying around in my head in ever anxiety-raising intensity. Had I correctly assessed her? Did she have meningococcal disease? How was she now? How could I ever forgive myself if she becomes seriously ill or even died? I simply could not get these thoughts out of my head. I had to know if she was alright.

At that time, serious infectious cases were reported on the news as community health alerts, so I decided to take my portable radio with us. Mark said, "Why are you taking a radio? You won't need it"! I knew *I* needed it so I dreamed up some vaguely plausible answer. During session breaks on the retreat I would sneak off and listen to it in our room to hear if there had been an outbreak of meningitis. By Sunday afternoon I was somewhat calmer and less anxiously distracted. I felt that 'enough' time had gone by without me hearing of a catastrophe happening in the life of this little girl for me to become less worried. I didn't need the reassurance of listening to the news anymore and I began to enjoy what was left of the retreat weekend. On Monday, back at school the very first thing I did was to go to her class and asked her teacher if she was okay—you know what the answer was!

THE TIRED-OUT BOY

In March 2001, we planned as a family to fly to Bangkok for a week's holiday, to assess an invitation my husband had received to move there for a two-year work contract. I could not wait to get away from all the pressures of my nurse role at school. I was constantly overly concerned about first aid decisions and as the end of each day approached I thought, "Sweet relief!" Alas, the day before the holidays started, a boy who had become over tired from running the school cross country race came to the sick bay. Although he was fine, just needing some TLC and a little rest before the drudgery of hitting classroom studies again, my mind began to obsess. "What if he has a previously undiagnosed heart condition? What if he has asthma and I've missed it? What if he was coming down with a fatal illness? How could I go overseas not knowing if he would recover? I knew I wouldn't be able to relax at all! If he is really sick and I have misdiagnosed him everyone will hate me, I'll be a social outcast, and I'll be seen as a failed Christian." I kept thinking that I should be a much better nurse.

I knew I was being irrational, but what could I do to reduce this all-consuming self-doubt? After the boy had rested and recovered I wrote a note for him to give to his mum, again as school protocol demanded, and sent him back to class. But when he left the sickbay I *really* began to worry. I thought to myself, "What if his mum doesn't get the note? What if it gets scrunched up in his school bag? What if he collapses before he gets home? How then will his parents know that he was unwell after the race? If things go pear-shaped it will all be my fault for not speaking to his parents." I tried to call his mum but could only leave an answering machine message. After I finished work that day I felt that the note and the one phone message were not enough. I tried to ring again when I was shopping for last minute holiday supplies and had to leave another message. So two phone messages and a note still was not sufficient for peace of mind.

In Bangkok, on our once in a lifetime family trip to this bustling and fascinating city, I could not stop worrying about this boy.

Dread (My Acute Illness)

My anxiety about him filled my mind. In every spare moment, I turned on the hotel TV to see if there were any headlines from Melbourne about a sick boy who had been mismanaged by the school nurse after a cross country race.

I asked Mark again and again what he thought of how I'd managed the situation at school, each time framing my question from a different angle. Did he think that the boy would be okay? Had I done everything humanly possible? An hour later I'd need to ask him the same questions again. (This behavior in OCD is called 'recruitment' where the sufferer can't find the reassurance they need so they obtain it from outside, by enlisting another person into the thought process). I tried hard to enjoy myself, but the nagging feeling of foreboding would not leave me for long. Now, 'best' wasn't good enough for me. It had to be perfect. Needless to say, when I went back to school I found the boy was just fine. At that point I realized I had to get out of that job. The healer had become sick.

In April 2001 I knew my obsessive worrying had become much worse. The straw that broke the camel's back was after I had a premonition. In the past I had very occasionally had 'prophetic' revelations, or if you like moments when I foresaw something that later took place. On this particular day, I had a premonition that two school boys would break their wrists and that, (if I wasn't careful), I would miss detecting this. I thought to myself, that even though this kind of mistake does happen, surely I couldn't be so dumb as to miss two fractures in one day? This must be my vivid imagination playing games with me. I put the premonition aside and carried on with my work.

Astonishingly, two boys did break their wrists that day, and I mistook both as sprains. With a cold shiver, I realized that my premonition had come true. What was God up to now? What kind of test was this? In my already highly anxious state, my brain went into overdrive, trying to cover all medical possibilities for each child who visited my sick bay from that day onward. In my mind the possibilities were all ominous; a schoolyard graze would result in getting the AIDS virus, a rash from rolling in the grass would become fatally anaphylactic and a splinter would develop into gangrene!

Finally, my brain was so full of obsessional thoughts that I could not think straight. I had completely lost trust in my professional judgement. For twenty years, I had made decisions rationally and calmly. Now I had lost that ability. I submitted my resignation, but as always wanting to do the right thing, I gave notice for the end of the school term. I wanted the principal to have plenty of time to find a new nurse. Because of this I had several weeks left to work. I dreaded every working day. Anxieties kept circumnavigating my mind, and this just added to the foreboding I felt as I had to face another day of work. I kept thinking, if only I can get through these last few days of work, everything will seem a piece of cake. I would then have time and space to figure myself out. I began counting down the days until I could leave.

I'll be leaving in two and a half weeks, but that's really only thirteen working days. Maybe, Rosemary, you won't get any more cases that freak you out. After all it's not as if you are working ten hour shifts. You only work four hours per day! Now that doesn't sound like a lot of time to hang in there, does it? You can do it! How hard can it be?

Irrationally, ridiculously, absurdly I was afraid of being the cause of death or permanent injury to a child, by making another wrong diagnosis, or failing in some catastrophic way. One very anxious thought that filled my mind was that people would come to hate me because of my mistakes. They would not know how deeply I cared about people in general and the children in my care at school. I was also afraid of being sued, arrested, and publicly humiliated for incompetence or overconfidence in my professional abilities. Possibly what worried me the most was the thought that my actions would result in the humiliation of my family. I would be seen as the incompetent nurse/mother who caused so much grief to the ones she loved. I thought, we will need to move interstate because of my mistakes and my husband and two children will lose everything because of me.

Dread (My Acute Illness)

I oscillated between the sensible professional woman who usually made good judgements, and the doubting irrational woman, pathologically questioning every one of her decisions. I came later to name this pathological self-doubter 'Gollum', the skulking character in J.R. Tolkien's 'Lord of the Rings'. He needled me with ridiculously implausible thoughts that my actions would have disastrous consequences. I was terrified. I couldn't shut him up. Gradually Gollum became a thug, dominating the sensible Rosemary, beating her into submission until she was overcome. Everything was obsessively doubted; the occasional obsession had become an everyday reality and the life was all but squeezed out of me.

I could no longer think straight. My mind was swamped by obsessional worries and fears. What do you do when you can't trust your own mind? I was checking and double checking and triple checking every decision I made. In my mind, I tried to cover all possible scenarios. When I say 'everything', I mean, everything. I began sending children home who didn't need to go, and not just one or two. I had lost trust in my professional judgements, and I never really found this trust again . . . This is where I began my story. On that day, walking from the compost bin in our backyard, I ran out of any emotional reserves. My tank was empty. I had run out of fuel. Although there were still several days left before the school term ended I rang the school office to tell them that I could not come to work anymore. In that moment, I knew I couldn't go on.

THE LAST STRAW

I rang my doctor's surgery for an urgent appointment. I needed a medical certificate. I don't remember a lot about that appointment but I know I blurted out many of my irrational fears and worries. "I'm not going back to work! I need a certificate! I think I'm going to get sued! I had a premonition that I'd miss two broken wrists and then I did miss them! What is more, I forgot to check the expiry dates on the school's new Ventolin inhalers that I just bought from the chemist. I mean, I checked the date on the outside of the boxes but I didn't open them up and check on the actual puffers themselves. If they have expired, then it's my fault because I should have checked the expiry dates on them. A child might die because they have expired and it'd be entirely my fault. A family will lose their child and blame me. I couldn't live with the guilt because despite the fact that I always try to do my best, I have really stuffed up."

My doctor, whom I'd known for several years, must have been very surprised to see me in this agitated and irrational state. He gently and carefully called it 'nervous exhaustion'. I thought to myself, "This is so foreign! This can't be happening! This is what other people do when they can't cope. This is not me."

I walked out of the clinic with a starter pack of anti-anxiety pills, an appointment to return in four days, and a blood test to be done. My doctor wanted to check for other medical conditions such as thyroid problems and anemia. If there was no improvement in four days, he would send me to a psychologist, and if there was still no improvement after three appointments, it would be off to a psychiatrist.

Physically I was suffering too. For months before I left work I had been distracting myself from my worries with 'comfort foods' and gained an extra eight kilograms of weight. And, as my worries evolved into irrational fears, I became constantly nauseous. My stomach was always in a knot and so then I began losing weight. Eventually I lost eleven kilograms and much of my body's iron stores. It required a series of iron injections to replenish my blood and it was months before I felt anywhere near normal physically.

PAPARAZZI

I rang my parents and blubbered, "I've cracked up"! They came right over and took me to the regional shopping center for lunch. We sat in the food hall, buzzing with life. I slumped in my chair, shoulders hunched, waiting for the police to tap me on the shoulder and arrest me for all the mistakes I'd made. In my mind, it was

Dread (My Acute Illness)

inevitable that they would turn up. It was just a question of time. It took months for me to realize that the police were never going to come for me. I had nothing to worry about with the law. The problems were in my mind.

I felt very guilty that I had let the school down by leaving before term ended, and I felt the school principal deserved an explanation for my abrupt departure. I visited him and apologized profusely, justifying my leaving the job early by explaining that it was due to my being anemic or possibly having thyroid trouble. He said, "It's stress." This annoyed me. I thought, "This isn't stress. I know what stress is. Whatever this is, it makes stress look like a picnic."

In the following days, I thought, "Okay, now I'm not employed anymore, I can figure out what's going on in my life." However, a few days later my children brought home the week's school newsletter and there it was, in glorious black and white. "Mrs Burke has found the duties of her position beyond her capacity to cope and has resigned." Now 'everyone' knew. No private breakdown, nothing hushed up, no face-saving exit from the school. Ours was a suburban primary school of 420 children. All I could think of was all those people knowing that I could not 'cope' with my job. I was a failure.

From then on whenever I went out, I felt that there was nowhere to hide. Walking the dog, picking up the children from school, going shopping, all made me incredibly anxious and guilt ridden. I felt humiliated. I was convinced I had let my family down. What a mess, I thought, and it's entirely my fault. It was not until months later that I accepted that all this was not my fault at all. My feelings were a result of a mental illness that had slowly taken over my life.

My life had unwound as if I had fumbled and dropped a reel of cotton. It sped across the table and rolled off, the last of the thread silently disappearing over the edge just as my hand slammed down to try to catch it. I had missed. It was gone, its escape route finally blocked at the skirting board where it stopped with a clunk. The unwound cotton lay amongst the floor dust. As I slowly wound it back onto its reel, I knew that it would never be as neat and tidy as it once was.

I described this image of how I felt to my friend Jeanette, who was to become the reviewer of the first draft of this book. In response, she wrote this encouraging poem for me.

Loose ends

> Lord, I like knots
> Tied securely and hard to undo.
> It satisfies me to tie them right,
> Each strand in its place
> No loose ends.
>
> Lord, I like bows,
> Ribbon tied purposefully,
> Creatively and beautifully,
> Firmly holding a present
> Or a shoe
>
> Or hair,
> Predictable and shapely,
> Pulled tightly to hold,
> No loose ends.
>
> Lord, I'm a tangle,
> A snarl of loose ends,
> Unfinished business,
> Unanswered questions,
> Wrongs to be righted,
> Tied off in a bow.
>
> I'm caught in the mysteries,
> Unexpected changes,
> Loose ends in my life

Dread (My Acute Illness)

The mess won't be ordered,
I struggle with failures,
Evil that won't be tied.

I see a cross
Covered with loose ends,
The horrible, unsorted mess
Of my failures,
Everyone's tangles,
Demanding retribution
And sorting

A tangled crown
Sharply presses down on Jesus' head
As he dies
For my loose ends

The price is paid,
The knot is tied,
As Jesus dies for me.
A gift is given
If I believe,
And bring my tangled mess.

The price is paid,
I take the gift
In trust,
A precious gift,
Tied with a glorious bow.

SEPTEMBER 2001
JEANETTE WOODS
USED WITH PERMISSION.

UNFAMILIAR TERRITORY

Several weeks later I was diagnosed as having Obsessive Compulsive Disorder (OCD). Yes, I knew that I had a tendency to be obsessive at times, but that was only when, for example, an exam was coming up or a music performance. On these occasions I would make sure the pegs all lined up on the clothes line and would fold the washing extra neatly. But not this! Not this debilitating worry. I didn't know what 'this' was; this endless "what if, what if, what if?" My diagnosis of OCD made sense. I had moved from being a little obsessive to a full-blown case of Obsessive Compulsive Disorder.

But there was more bad news. My psychiatrist also diagnosed me with depression. He said OCD and depression often go together. I thought, "No I'm not depressed!" Then I realized "*Oh yes I am!*" I felt hopelessly lost in a horrible black cave. But slowly, I started to address these feelings that I'd been denying for months.

At this point of time I felt a real failure. People like me don't crack up! I am a Christian! I am a nurse! I am not weak! I have it sorted! And I kept asking myself, "How could I have been so stupid? Why did this happen to me? What on earth am I supposed to do with my life now"? Today I have answers to these questions. Importantly, now I say, "Why not? It's an illness. Like all illnesses, it can happen to anyone, men and women, Christians and non-Christians, nurses and doctors."

What I had to accept and internalize was that Christians can get mentally ill. I had not failed as a Christian because I had OCD and depression. Our faith in Christ, no matter how important and real it is to us does not shield us from illnesses of any kind. Yes, God answers prayer and prayer is always part of the healing process. Sometimes Christians find miraculous healing solely through prayer, but miracles are by definition, something exceptional. I believe in miraculous healing but not that everyone when they pray will be miraculously healed. In most cases when we become sick, our illness follows its natural course, during which we may need to seek medical help. My error had been to mistake a mental illness as entirely a spiritual illness. Today I am thankful for the wonderful

Dread (My Acute Illness)

help my doctors provided, but I am more thankful to God for getting me through my illness and making me the person I now am. I know he answered my prayers. Yes, it was my mind that got sick but in the healing of my mind I also found spiritual healing. I think I am a more open minded and compassionate human being because of this experience. God used my suffering constructively. My journey has been a faith journey.

So the story I now bring to you is not a text book, nor a self-help guide. Yes, I will draw on experts to help explain terminology to bring accurate insights where needed, because my heartfelt aim is to help destigmatize OCD and bring a message of hope. But essentially, it's my journey through illness, diagnosis, management and recovery as a Christian with OCD. I hope you'll join me as I retell it.

2.

Disequilibrium (The Diagnosis)

FOR A PERSON WITH a healthy mind it can be very difficult to understand the struggles of someone with an unhealthy one. The friend or loved one with clinical depression, for example, is a worrying puzzle. We may ask ourselves, "Why don't they just 'buck up' and think positively? Why are they so lethargic? Why can't they embrace all the good things in their lives"? Nothing physical is wrong with them and yet they may appear to us as if they have a rain cloud hanging over them wherever they go.

OCD is just as perplexing. It defies our common sense. Why, we ask, don't they stop washing their hands, obsessively worrying about everything and being constantly stressed lest they let someone down? It's behaviors like this that have given OCD the nickname the disease of 'pathological doubt'.

There are two paths to understanding these disturbances of the mind, in this case specifically OCD. We can read the professional literature that seeks to explain what is taking place in the life of the person with abnormal behavior and a troubled mind, and we can listen to those who can tell us what it is like to have OCD. In this chapter I invite you to come with me as I lead you down these two avenues. I will recount what I have learnt from the experts on OCD, and I will tell you a little of my story. I will give the facts and I will tell you of my obsessive and compulsive feelings. In

DISEQUILIBRIUM (THE DIAGNOSIS)

both cases the information will not exactly correspond with what you or someone else you know with OCD has experienced because no two people have the exact same experiences. In all of this, it is very important to remember that OCD is a recognized and treatable illness.

WHAT IS THIS ILLNESS?

First, here is an explanation and description from psychologist Patrick McGrath in *The OCD Answerbook* that I have found helpful. He defines OCD as an anxiety disorder and goes on to explain that:

> Anxiety disorders make their sufferers feel disproportionately anxious or fearful, and the main anxiety triggers for people with OCD are obsessive thoughts, images, or impulses that are intrusive and inappropriate and that cause a great deal of distress. They are obsessive because they are unwanted, and a person experiences them over and over again. As a response to these obsessions, a person performs compulsive behaviors in an attempt to somehow get rid of or neutralize the obsessions. Further, these compulsive behaviors go well beyond what would be necessary in everyday life to actually deal with the themes of the obsessive thoughts, impulses or images. Unfortunately, the compulsions relieve the anxiety only temporarily, and the obsessions return, causing the cycle to play over and over again throughout the day . . . These obsessions can occur ten to twenty-five times a day, or even more frequently, and the compulsive behaviors that follow help the person relieve the anxiety brought on by the thought. The behavior is very excessive, however, and seems to work only for a short period of time. Then the obsessions typically return, and the cycle starts all over again.[1]

In my own words, after years of thinking about OCD, I explain it this way. Most of us have compulsive and obsessive feelings from time to time, even in some cases quite often. Who has not had a restless night worrying about the consequences of an assignment

1. McGrath, *The OCD Answerbook*, 2.

that is overdue, or an upsetting conflict at work or whether we left the iron on when we went off for a night away. And many, if not most of us, have some routine behavior, even a peculiar one! My friend's mother always had to have the milk in the cup before pouring the tea. She could not enjoy her cuppa if this rule was broken. I know of someone who has to get dressed before they leave their bedroom. To do otherwise would be felt to be wrong. These things are not OCD. OCD goes well beyond normal worries and pedantic habits. It involves besieging thoughts and distressing urges to repeat behaviors; it stifles spontaneity and steals the joy of living. It is human behavior rife with fears, behaviors and thinking that are compulsive, unrelenting and irresistible to the sufferer. It can be explained in terms of common human experience, but the mental state and the behavior that results from it is not normal. It is off the scale completely of what may be considered 'normal'.

The burned letters

Here is a personal story to explain what I am saying. In the week after I left my school job, I sent six letters to the school office staff to tell them of my Health Centre activities that I had not been able to complete before I unceremoniously left my job. Why so many? I felt compelled to make sure that the school knew everything that I had been doing in the Health Centre. At all costs, I wanted to avoid any distress or harm that might come to a child because of my absence. All I could think about was the instructions I needed to pass on to make sure the school knew what needed to be done. I wanted to cover every possibility. And at the back of my mind was the dread of letting my family down.

My daughter was the courier of all these letters, delivering them to the office staff for action. After several days of deliveries, she returned from school and gently told me that the office staff had had enough of my pedantic letters and that they said that they were more than capable of running a sickbay whilst awaiting a replacement for me. Embarrassed, annoyed and frustrated, I had to accept that things were beyond my control.

Disequilibrium (The Diagnosis)

But then I began obsessing again. I had labored over every word of those six letters, producing and printing out various draft versions until I got them perfectly composed. Those drafts were then screwed up and tossed in my waste paper basket. How should I discard these? If I put them in the garbage bin outside, would someone read them? What if one of these letters blew out of the bin when the garbage truck was emptying it? If I tore them up, could someone glue them back together again and identify the children I was referring to? What if that became a breach of confidentiality on my part? I decided that I had better burn the drafts. And so I burned them on the concrete back veranda on a windless day.

After the little fire was out, I was relieved and went back inside the house. But unfortunately, I heard someone saying on the radio that fires can start in the eaves of houses. On hearing this I then feared that the little glowing embers from my tiny pyre of letters would float past the three sides of our home and set our neighbor's house on fire! Maybe the embers would glow for days biding their time for that ideal opportunity to be fanned into flame. Would the house burn down and my neighbors die? I rang my husband Mark in tears and sought his reassurance. He was amazingly reassuring. In those early days, it didn't matter what time it was, I would ring Mark in Bangkok or Jakarta or wherever he was for his assurance. Sometimes I would ring him twice about the same worry. I would sit on the couch in tears, fretting over my obsessions. In an effort to comfort me, my daughter brought me a blanket more than once. I was ashamed that it was not the other way around; the mother comforting the child.

I spent the next five days worrying that the neighbor's house would burn down. It is still there, more than fifteen years later. This is what OCD is like. So often sufferers are so ashamed of their behavior they try to hide it.

In their very helpful self-help book, *Brain Lock,* authors Jeffrey Schwartz and Beverley Beyette explain how extreme some compulsive behavior can become:

> The victims of OCD engage in bizarre and self-destructive behaviors to avert some imagined catastrophe. But

there is no realistic connection between the behaviors and the catastrophes they so fear. For example, they may shower 40 times a day to "ensure" that there will not be a death in the family. Or they may go to great lengths to avoid certain numbers so as to "prevent" a fatal airplane crash. Unlike compulsive shoppers or compulsive gamblers, people with OCD derive no pleasure from performing the rituals. They find them extremely painful.[2]

OCD is not 'normal' thinking and behaving, even if it has some counterpart in how we can sometimes think and behave. It is an awful illness that takes over someone's life and makes them feel powerless to resist its diabolic control. Perhaps now you can see why shame and secretiveness can cover up this disorder for years.

STATISTICS

The importance of knowing more about OCD is highlighted by the statistics.

> Obsessive Compulsive Disorder (OCD) affects 2-3 percent of the population—more than 500,000 Australians. OCD has been recognized as the fourth most common psychiatric disorder after phobias, substance abuse and major depression. OCD usually begins in late childhood or early adolescence.[3]

At first, we might think 2-3 percent of the population is not that great a number, but when you realize this works out to be 2-3 people in every one hundred, 20-30 in every one thousand people and in excess of half a million Australians, we realize it's magnitude. To help us visualize just how many people OCD impacts on, let's think Australia's most iconic sports stadium, The Melbourne Cricket Ground (MCG). Its spectator capacity is up to 100,000. Statistically, four seating bays worth of those keen spectators would have OCD. Australia's largest club, the Melbourne Cricket Club,

---

2. Schwartz, *Brain Lock*, xiii.
3. Anxiety Recovery Centre, *Obsessive Compulsive Disorder OCD*, lines 1-3.

DISEQUILIBRIUM (THE DIAGNOSIS)

has an MCG Members' Reserve Stand that seats almost 23,000. It's a lavish part of the MCG, with bars, dining rooms and cafes. When I have sat watching in the public stands at cricket matches, I have gazed enviously over the hallowed turf to the Members' Reserve. Statistically those who have OCD would take up a whole bay of that luxurious stand! An amazing statistic related to the MCG is that there are 217,000 people waiting to join the Melbourne Cricket Cub! (Some parents add their children's names to the membership waiting list at birth because the wait is well over 10 years!) 5,500 of those patient people, waiting years for a membership place to become available, would have OCD at any one time.

It doesn't matter where we live in the world, our background or what our socio-economic standing is, OCD can be found. Even amongst the passionate cricket fans in India, OCD would be present in roughly the same percentage. This means that 2,250 of the 90,000 enthusiastic fans watching a match at Eden Gardens Stadium in Kolkata, India would have OCD.

Patrick McGrath says,

> OCD is a very serious disorder. In fact, of all the mental health disorders, it is considered one of the most serious in terms of the amount of burden it causes the population of the world, according to the World Health Organization. This is a result of several factors, including the number of people who are affected by it . . . the ability of OCD to affect people across the age spectrum (from children through senior citizens), the difficulty in finding specialized treatment, and the often-devastating effects it can have on people who suffer from it.[4]

OBSESSIONS AND COMPULSIONS

Very early on in my treatment, my psychiatrist recommended that I get in touch with The Anxiety Recovery Centre of Victoria (ARCVic). A Victorian community mental health organization,

---

4. McGrath, *The OCD Answerbook*, 7.

ARCVic provides support, self-help, recovery, early intervention and educational services to people and families living with anxiety disorders. They proved to be, and still are extremely helpful, and I continue to receive their newsletters. ARCVic explains OCD in this way:

> People with OCD experience recurrent and persistent thoughts, images or impulses that are intrusive and unwanted (obsessions), and perform repetitive and ritualistic behaviors that are excessive, time consuming and distressing (compulsions). Common obsessions include fears of contamination and fears of harm to self or others. Common compulsions include excessive hand washing, showering, checking and repeating rituals. These compulsions and obsessions may take up many hours of a person's day. OCD can cause significant interference in family and social relationships, and daily routines, and may intrude into every activity and action.

Many people with OCD experience intense fears of something terrible happening to themselves or others, they have constant doubts about their behavior, and frequently seek reassurance from others. Prior to identification and treatment of the disorder, families may become deeply involved in the sufferer's rituals, causing significant distress and disruption to all members of the family.

> People with OCD are typically aware of the irrationality and excessive nature of their compulsive behaviors and obsessive thoughts. They feel unable to control the obsessions or effectively limit their intrusiveness. Compulsions mostly develop into highly complex rituals, which cause high levels of frustration and anxiety for the sufferer. People with OCD are often acutely embarrassed about their symptoms and may keep them a secret for years, at times even from close friends and family. Those affected can live in their own private hell for years, while outwardly seeming to cope with and lead a relatively normal life. However, this seeming normality is only maintained at great cost in time, energy, stress and personal effort . . . It is a distressing and debilitating condition, which tends

to be chronic and deteriorate without appropriate treatment and support.⁵

In seeking to understand this *dis-ordering* of the mind the two key terms, 'obsession' and 'compulsion' need to be discussed.

The word 'Obsession'

Schwartz defines 'obsession' in reference to OCD this way.

> Obsessions are intrusive, unwelcome, distressing thoughts and mental images. The word *obsession* comes from the Latin word meaning "to besiege". And an obsessive thought is just that—a thought that besieges you and annoys the hell out of you. You pray for it to go away, but it won't, at least not for long or in any controllable way. These thoughts always create distress and anxiety. Unlike other unpleasant thoughts, they do not fade away but keep intruding into your mind over and over, against your will. These thoughts are, in fact, repugnant to you."⁶

On reading this vivid description of the nature of obsessive thoughts, we catch a glimpse of just how debilitating OCD can be. The sufferer feels bound by obsessions and can't dismiss them. Here are some examples:

- The need to say, collect or remember things
- Fear of touching something because it might have germs
- Thoughts and anxieties about food being contaminated
- Doubts about having not done something, for example turning off the oven
- Upsetting ideas, thoughts or pictures that come into mind repeatedly
- Fear of driving lest you kill someone

---

5. Anxiety Recovery Centre, *Obsessive Compulsive Disorder OCD,* lines 4–21.
6. Schwartz, *Brain Lock,* xiv.

- The need for order or symmetry
- Disgust with normal bodily functions
- An unrealistic sense of responsibility

For several weeks after I left my school position, I would spend much of the day dreading going to collect the children from school. I would curl up on the couch for hours, trying to distract myself from obsessing about my fears. I would do crosswords, read magazines or try to doze, seeking to quell my fears and to help the time pass. My obsessions were paralyzing.

The word 'Compulsion'

Jeffrey Schwartz defines this term in reference to OCD in this way:

> Compulsions are the behaviors that people with OCD perform in a vain attempt to exorcise the fears and anxieties caused by their obsessions. Although a person with OCD usually recognizes that the urge to wash, check, or touch things or to repeat numbers is ridiculous and senseless, the feeling is so strong that *the untrained mind* becomes overwhelmed and the person with OCD gives in and performs the compulsive behavior. Unfortunately performing the absurd behavior tends to set off a vicious cycle: it may bring momentary relief, but as more compulsive behaviors are performed, the obsessive thoughts and feelings become stronger, more demanding, and more tenacious.[7]

Someone with OCD may feel compelled to perform compulsions such as:

- Repeating certain routine activities
- Touching and tapping
- Rigidly placing objects according to rules and patterns
- Constantly asking certain questions
- Confessing their activities or thoughts

7. Schwartz, *Brain Lock*, xvi.

- Counting and repeating words
- Hand washing, washing clothes, food, household items, showering even for hours for fear of contamination or passing on a contamination.
- Checking locks, light switches, knowing that you have just checked them, to be sure you or others are safe.
- Continually correcting homework until it feels just right
- Some compulsions are hidden or performed as silent repetitive mental acts e.g. praying, counting.

Behaviors like these can interfere with life in many ways. Some find that spending so much time on compulsive behaviors results in them being chronically late for work or late in handing in study assignments. Reading becomes difficult due to the abnormal urge to review or reread or check previous pages and chapters. Skin irritation can develop from repetitive hand washing.

The school bunny

One of my most embarrassing OCD incidents provides another classic example of this illness. Just before I left my job, a little girl came to the sick bay. She had been given a little nip on her finger by the school rabbit. It was a tiny bite that didn't even break the skin and reassurance was all that was necessary in a sensible world. But not in my OCD world. I thought her mother needs to know about this bite in case it turns into tetanus and the little girl dies (obsession). I wrote a note for her to take home to her mum (compulsion), and she went away happy. But that wasn't enough for me. I began to worry. What if she loses the note? What if her mum doesn't realize the risks of this animal bite? What if it gets infected? (obsession).

So, I rang the home phone number and her grandma picked up the phone. I left a message with her (compulsion) which she assured me she would deliver to her daughter. But 45 minutes later I had my doubts. What if Grandma didn't tell the mum? (obsession). So,

I rang again (compulsion). This time Grandma was a little terse in replying. "No", she said, "I will not forget to pass on your message, thank you very much." I knew what I'd done was really stupid and I felt such a dill. At this stage I really was beginning to run out of all emotional reserves and my coping mechanisms were failing badly.

Scrupulosity—a common form of OCD

For some OCD suffers, scrupulosity is another form of this illness. This word also needs definition. One meaning for the word scrupulous is "having scruples: having or showing a strict regard for what is right."[8]. Many people are driven to do the right thing, especially many Christians, but in OCD scrupulosity is of a tyrannical kind. The feeling that you must always do the right thing; that you must never let God down; that you must live up to the expectations you think others have of you, fills your mind. In my case this drive to do the right thing had always been part of me, but when I became ill that drive became distressing.

Laurie Krauth in her insightful article, "Scrupulosity: Blackmailed by OCD in the name of God"[9] explains things very well:

> Sufferers of scrupulosity around the world [experience] nightmarish thoughts. They have persistent, irrational, unwanted beliefs and thoughts about not being devout or moral enough, despite all evidence to the contrary. They believe they have or will sin, disappoint God, or be punished for failing. In response to their disturbing thoughts, they try to calm themselves by using a host of compulsions. Some repeat religious phrases; others call their pastors for reassurance. Many avoid situations—even their beloved church or temple—because it triggers their horrible obsessive thoughts...
> SCRUPULOSITY VERSUS HEALTHY MORAL AND RELIGIOUS BELIEF. If you have an occasional

---

8. Delbridge, Bernard, Blair, Butler, Peters and Yallop, *The Macquarie Dictionary Revised Third Edition*, 1698.

9. Krauth, "Scrupulosity: Blackmailed by OCD in the name of God," lines 27-32, 68-70 and 231-232. Used with permission.

irrational, unwanted thought, do you have OCD? Everyone has such thoughts; people without OCD just dismiss them as unimportant and move on. If you are committed to your religion, morality, or ethics, and want to be as good as you can be, is this scrupulosity? Many devout and good people feel this way, and continually demand more of themselves, but they don't have OCD. People without OCD may try harder when they feel guilt or disappointment about something they think or do. But they are not obsessed with their failure.

OCD sufferers, on the other hand, dramatically overreact to perceived failures. They "see sin where there is none"[10] (Nelson, Abramowitz, Whiteside and Deacon, 2006) or blame themselves for falling short of impossibly high standards. They are tortured by the intensity of their doubts about their goodness, and the belief that, therefore, they are downright bad.

. . . Examples of other religions with beliefs and practices that can be mistaken for scrupulosity abound. But the anguished obsessions and compulsions, the tormenting doubt and guilt distinguish scrupulosity sufferers from morally and religiously inspired people.

Krauth goes on to describe the successful treatment for a client (patient) who was suffering this form of OCD and most importantly, finishes her article saying,

"The bottom line is that people with scrupulosity can maintain their faith and stop being blackmailed by their OCD."

The first recorded case of OCD was as early as the Spanish Inquisition[11], when a monk was investigated by the tribunal as he had blasphemous thoughts in church. The diagnosis was made retrospectively.

    10. Nelson, Abramowitz, Whiteside and Deacon, "Scrupulosity in patients with obsessive–compulsive disorder: Relationship to clinical and cognitive phenomena", 20.

    11. In the late 15th Century, the Monarchs of Spain initiated a tribunal be set up to investigate cases that their Roman Catholic Church considered of heresy or a similar offense. This is known as "the Spanish Inquisition".

MY TEENAGE YEARS—EVIDENCE OF EARLY ANXIETY

My personal story illustrates how OCD symptoms can evolve out of tendencies we have in our own personality. In my teenage years, for reasons I will outline below, I became quite scrupulous. I was driven to do the right thing but not in any obsessive way. After I left school this trait subsided but years later it suddenly developed a life of its own and possessed me.

I was a happy, mostly carefree girl up to the age of twelve. I loved climbing our large garden trees and frequently ventured onto the roof of our house and garage. I played with gangly spiders, wood lice and caterpillars, rode my bike flat out, swung on my swing, hoping it would go around full circle! I loved going to Sunday school, listening to the Bible stories and watching them be illustrated on the fuzzy felt board. For the good of the world and Jesus, I decided that I should be very well behaved. (Of course, this was frequently not the case! Tantrums and huffiness were not in short supply! Who can sustain such a vow?). I sat in church services trying to look angelic and pondered their somberness and length!

With fascination and a yearning to be like them, I observed my three older siblings navigating their way through their teenage years. I was desperate to be old enough to start Secondary School and, like my sisters, travel on the train and tram in that fantastic school uniform with the hat, blazer and badge.

Finally, I was old enough and started in grade 7. It was a great adventure. It took me and my friends a few days before we were game to venture out of the grade 7 building grounds and into the maze that was the large girls' college that I was attending. Unfortunately, after a few months I began to feel physically unwell. I was frequently nauseated and tired all the time. I wondered what had happened to my energy levels. I wasn't the energetic kid I had been. Sometimes I had a mild fever alongside these vague symptoms. The answer came when just before I turned twelve, I was diagnosed with glandular fever.

Disequilibrium (The Diagnosis)

Over the eight weeks I missed from school, some friends joked and asked me to confess who I had been kissing. Glandular fever is known as the 'Kissing Disease' because it is usually transmitted by saliva. No one was allowed to go near me or even sit on my bed, lest they catch it. I remember one lady visiting me and, whilst my mother was out of the room making her a cup of tea, she tried to cajole me into saying whom I had kissed. She said that it was bad to keep secrets from your parents. But the fact was, I was a good girl and I hadn't kissed anyone. This 'Kissing Disease' was not my fault and to prove it, I would become an even better-behaved girl.

Confused and sapped of enough energy even to walk across our lounge room, I asked Dad whether if I read a Psalm every night, it would stop me from vomiting. He said "Darling, it doesn't work that way." I was desperate to have control over this thing that made me feel nauseated all the time, and annoyed that people thought I had got it because I had kissed someone. I also hated vomiting!

After seven weeks away from school with glandular fever I was admitted to hospital for a complete check-up. I was insulted by being put in the children's ward and I cried my heart out in the ward toilet! I was so miserable after being sick for so long. What on earth had happened to me, I asked myself. The nurse was dismayed. I had locked the toilet door and wouldn't open it. Through the locked door she scolded me, telling me to pull myself together because I would upset the other children. I didn't care. Nobody seemed to care about me. Why was I struck down with this awful illness and stigmatized by its reputation?

The specialist told my parents to send me back to school, regardless of a persistent fever. No longer infectious, it was doing me more harm than good to stay isolated at home. However, the girl who went back to school was not the same one who had started so happily earlier that year.

The day that I returned, my school friends had set up a welcome back party for me, but I couldn't bring myself to eat the beautiful chocolate cake they had baked, because I was afraid I would get food poisoning and vomit and become sick all over again. My friends were puzzled and disappointed, and told me so.

From then on and for quite a long time, I held my school lunch sandwiches in torn off shreds of cling wrap. Fearful of being coughed on, I refused to go to the shopping center for several weeks. These behaviors gradually disappeared but were replaced by others that earned me a reputation for being 'odd' and a 'goody two-shoes'. These were motivated by my quest to re-establish myself as 'good', to rid myself of the Kissing Disease reputation.

So, I resolved to be the perfectly behaved child, especially at school. Summer uniform hats had been abolished but I was the only one of all the school girls to still wear one. The top buttons of our dresses were to be done up and I was one of the few that rigidly kept this rule. My socks were always pulled up and I had no 'dog ate my homework' excuses for late assignments. My classroom behavior was A+, no demerits or detentions for me. I had to strive for perfection.

Throughout my secondary school years my compulsions waxed and waned. They were never all consuming, but always lurking in the background. When an exam was approaching they would become worse, but when the pressure was over, things returned to an acceptable normality. Nevertheless, I could never go to sleep without my favorite toys' ears flipped down and my crocheted rug the right way up. I would scribble out words that I had written until they felt 'right'. My personal diary always had to be signed off with six kisses. I would have to play the same piano piece repeatedly until I did it perfectly— if I made a mistake, I would begin again right from the start, much to my family's exasperation. At home I would unwind from the relentless pressure I put myself under at school, with teenage tantrums, door slamming and self-loathing. When my schooling was finally completed, I was greatly relieved.

HOW IS OCD DIAGNOSED?

OCD needs to be distinguished from other conditions that may share some of its signs and symptoms. During a consultation, a clinician commonly uses an approved and standard diagnostic questionnaire to assist in diagnosis. They go through the questions with their patient, giving a rating to the answers and then use these results as part of their diagnostic process. They ask about medical history, explore habits, and take a family history of any mental illnesses. In my case, diagnosis took a few weeks. From my local doctor I went to a psychologist who tried treating my symptoms. She sought to help me with relaxation techniques. When I did not get any better my local doctor referred me on to a psychiatrist. After three consultations involving me outlining my family history, telling him of my symptoms, an interview with my husband Mark and a detailed questionnaire, he made the diagnosis of OCD.

HOW IS OCD TREATED?

As I began to adjust to my diagnosis and begin the long trek back to health, I learned that the treatment of OCD usually involves a range of strategies. It was not treated by just taking a 'happy pill' and getting on with life. A multi-faceted approach was what worked best. Standard approaches include Cognitive Behavioral Therapy (CBT), where the psychiatrist helps you think more rationally about your fears and obsessions; group therapy where you share with other OCD sufferers in a group chaired by someone who understands the illness well in a professional capacity; anxiety management, which can include breathing exercises and mindfulness; and medication that can quieten the symptoms. In the recovery process, a support group and education is beneficial. Different combinations of strategies work for different people.

For me, Cognitive Behavioral Therapy, medication, anxiety management and education about the disorder was the combination that helped straighten out my thought processes. As my story unfolds, I will outline more on all this. In the case of Anxiety Disorders, the word 'recovery' is much more appropriate than 'cure'. This is how ARCVic describes recovery on their website;

> Recovery involves gaining quality of life through meaningful roles, relationships, and participation in the community. Recovery is less about cure and more about

living a satisfying life. There will inevitably be times throughout recovery when your progress dips, or even regresses. Relapses are a part of recovery, and instead of viewing these backward steps as a 'failure', it is important to recognize them as an opportunity to learn about yourself. By doing this you can effectively determine your triggers in order to better handle future situations.

Just as living with anxiety is an individual experience, the process of recovery means different things to different people. While you may not return to full health, you will gain an ability to manage symptoms so that they do not interfere with everyday activities.[12]

Did I want a cure for my condition? Of course I wanted a cure! I wanted to be a different person. But that was not going to happen. I was me and I had to learn simply to be a better functioning me. I had to learn that the future for me was being Rosemary who was a wiser, more compassionate, less anxious, less self-driven person who found joy in life. In the next part of my story, I'd like to tell you my motivations for revealing my experiences as an OCD sufferer. Much of my motivation comes because I want to share with you how God gave me precious pearls of wisdom, encouragement and acceptance along my convoluted path through treatment to recovery. It is my prayer that what I disclose with some pain may help someone else.

---

12. Anxiety Recovery Centre, *What is recovery?* lines 1–10.

3.

Darkness (Having Depression)

IN MY FIRST TWO chapters I wrote about events that led up to my diagnosis of OCD and explained what OCD is. I am now going to expand on my experiences in the first few months after this diagnosis. It was a gloomy, unsettling time for me because not only did I have OCD but also major depression. Not everyone with OCD has depression and not everyone with depression has OCD. But in the early days after diagnosis, I experienced both. Thus for me there were two related conditions to treat and learn to manage.

There are four parts to this chapter: I will describe how OCD wore me down to the point of not functioning properly in everyday life; I will define depression; I will talk about how hurtful and confusing it was to find fellow Christians judging me as weak in faith because I had a mental illness and lastly, I will share a poem I wrote when I was sickest, about finding myself in a cave while out bushwalking.

NOT FUNCTIONING

When I met my psychiatrist for the first time, he suggested that at the next appointment, I bring my husband Mark with me. He said talking with Mark would help him confirm his diagnosis of OCD as well as help him understand our situation as a family.

At this appointment, he said to me, "We are aiming in the short term to get you back to a point where you can function." I realized that this meant I was *not* functioning normally. "Wow" I said to myself. "He is suggesting I am 'not functioning'. How can this be me? And yet now I realize that it *is* me, because I'm so obsessed about everything that I can't behave normally."

The psychiatrist went on to prescribe medication. Specific anti-anxiety medications are usually a significant tool in managing OCD, but these medications take several weeks to begin to have a good effect. I was not well enough, he said, to begin to tackle OCD with other therapies until my medication had begun to work. Having to wait weeks for this was extremely difficult. How could I survive the torture for that long? When would I have some relief from so many obsessive thoughts?

I was exhausted by all the anxious and compulsive feelings that filled my mind. My concentration was almost non-existent. I needed to use the oven timer to remind myself to depart for appointments I had made. I would forget what I was talking about in the middle of a sentence. And the efficiency with which I normally executed tasks, a fact on which I prided myself, had disappeared. I was nervously jumpy and wondered how I would ever cope with life's challenges and inevitable failures again. I would ruminate over possible disastrous scenarios for even the smallest of decisions I made. I could not think rationally—common sense had gone out the window. If there was a one in a million chance that I might do something wrong, even inadvertently, then I believed that it would happen. My imagination began to play tricks on me. For example, after an absolutely uneventful drive home I would imagine that I had hit someone, and would listen to the radio news for word of the accident. There hadn't been an accident. I knew that, but I couldn't stop myself from worrying about it. Did I pull out too fast in front of those cars—did they have an accident after I had gone out of sight, because of me? I desperately needed to know.

I was so fearful of many things in the early days after my 'breakdown' that a few times I curled up in the fetal position and rocked in overwhelming distress. Thinking back on this time,

Darkness (Having Depression)

I now recognize that this is what people do when uncontrolled thoughts overwhelm them. Like the terrified victims of Pompeii in 79AD when Mt. Vesuvius erupted and buried them in toxic ash, I felt completely buried by fear.

I became so tired of analyzing everything. Almost everything worried me in some way or another. The things that normally blur into the background because the brain filters them out remained at the front of my brain. I continually analyzed and thought about people's expressions, words, mannerisms and so on. Conversations went on around me but I was not able to participate in them. I was self-absorbed with my own overwhelming sense of responsibility. I was completely worn out and couldn't face making eye contact.

I had a very low threshold for coping with everyday tasks and my 'fight or flight response' released adrenaline many times a day. There was no variation in the degree of what was significant when *everything* felt significant. From putting away a knife in a kitchen drawer, to receiving a phone call, I visualized my brain as being like the fused mess of a melted electrical power board after a power overload.

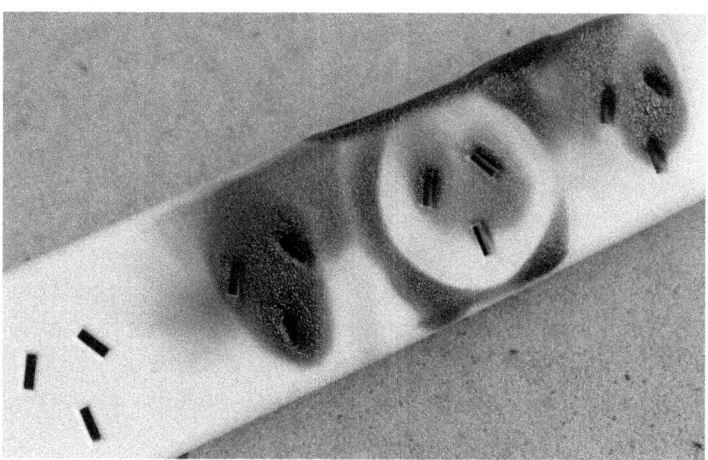

Melted Power Board

As I struggled to become calmer and more rational, I was desperate for my next psychiatric appointment where I could tell my doctor of my struggles. The wait in between each appointment was excruciating. One morning at 3.30 am, unable to sleep, as I longed for the day I would see my psychiatrist I wrote this:

I feel like a new born lamb; it's so hard to stand up that I frequently fall over. I leap vertically at small stimuli. I guess this translates into trying to live, implementing what I'm learning. Getting involved again even on a small scale. Making mistakes, saying the wrong thing, getting mixed up, feeling like a court jester, the fool, a lot. But mostly trying not to be an adrenaline junkie. The absence of fear. Like the eye of a storm. Peaceful! But the cyclone of life rotates around me and it cannot be avoided.

My psychiatrist gave me several simple distraction strategies to reduce anxiety, but my mind was so cluttered that at first I did not do very well with them. As for ever returning to work, I couldn't imagine being responsible for anything more than washing tea towels. One distraction I was able to implement was visiting our Council library, which became a great 'friend'. Here I found picture books, craft books, and light reading magazines to read that helped overcome the awful thoughts that overwhelmed my thinking.

I called these early days of not functioning the 'shaky days'. Sometimes a shaky day began when I was genuinely happy and peaceful, then metaphorically walked into a street pole of obsession. I remembered again my 'breakdown' at work and I felt ashamed. I wanted to accept what had happened without feeling sorry for myself, but the ability to do so was missing. I needed time out until these terrible feelings subsided. Sometimes they manifested themselves when I'd dared to be excited about the future but then wilted as the reality of the present overwhelmed. I would cry out silently, "God *please* heal me."

Rich Mullins, a contemporary Christian singer/songwriter wrote this prayer song that I could really relate to on days like these:

DARKNESS (HAVING DEPRESSION)

Hold me Jesus[1]

Sometimes my life just don't make sense at all
When the mountains look so big
And my faith just seems so small

So hold me Jesus 'cause I'm shaking like a leaf
You have been King of my glory
Won't You be my Prince of Peace

And I wake up in the night and feel the dark
It's so hot inside my soul
I swear there must be blisters on my heart

So hold me Jesus 'cause I'm shaking like a leaf
You have been King of my glory
Won't You be my Prince of Peace

Surrender don't come natural to me
I'd rather fight You for something I don't really want
Than to take what You give that I need
And I've beat my head against so many walls
I'm falling down I'm falling on my knees

And this Salvation Army band is playing this hymn
And Your grace rings out so deep
It makes my resistance seem so thin

So hold me Jesus 'cause I'm shaking like a leaf
You have been King of my glory
Won't You be my Prince of Peace

---

1. Rich Mullins, *Hold Me Jesus* Copyright ©1993 Universal Music—Brentwood Benson Publ. Used with permission.

DEPRESSION

The word "depression" means different things to different people. The medical illness Depression is not the same as experiencing a day every now and then of low, down or sad mood. It is more persistent than that. There is a range of depressive illness types and levels of severity. Importantly, there has been and continues to be much expert research into depression. This has led to many effective treatment strategies, crisis support and excellent resources to aid recovery.

Emeritus Professor Sidney Bloch in "Understanding Troubled Minds" says that

> There is no precise dividing line between ordinary sadness and what psychiatrists call clinical depression. We use this term when lowered mood persists, brings intense distress, and interferes with the person's ability to cope with the ordinary demands of living, whether of work, study or personal relationships. This lack of a clear division is typical of many areas or our mental health.[2]

What I experienced

Depression clouded much of my early recovery process. It is hard to write about and it *is* very hard to explain what I went through. But I write my story in the hope that it will help someone on the path back to a non-depressed and fulfilling life.

Week after week at our church home group meetings I would sit on the couch beside Mark and barely be able to hold a conversation with my friends. I felt faded and tired with my own personal dark rain cloud shadowing me everywhere I went. I was pursued by the inescapable disappointment that my life would never be the same again. This is how I would describe my constant thought: *"Someone else has the ticket for my place in the life queue but when did I hand over mine? I didn't intend to! I wish I hadn't because I fear I will not get another turn."*

---

2. Bloch, *Understanding Troubled Minds*. 83.

Darkness (Having Depression)

Plagued with feelings of guilt, failure and foolishness, my mood swings were startling in their severity. One morning, I walked out of church in the middle of the service without telling Mark that I wasn't coming back. I intended to walk all the way to 'wherever' or drop before I got there. However, I soon changed my mind and went home to sleep. Mark was justifiably very angry with me. I hadn't answered his worried text messages asking me to explain where I'd gone. "Never do that again!" he said with exasperation, but at the time I didn't care what he thought. I felt as if I had become a melancholy drama queen who was consumed by her own worries.

One weekend Mark dropped me at our regional shopping center. I planned to catch the bus home. Instead I walked the seven kilometers home, crying all the way for all passers-by to see. What I remember of that day is profound grief. Grief over what I perceived I had lost.

Cranky and irritable, I overreacted to many things—even Mark's facial expressions during our conversations. I would misinterpret them and use them as fodder for my bonfire of self-loathing. I slammed doors and even deliberately broke a coffee cup in front of him. I did not intend that our eight-year-old daughter see this, but she did and still remembers it as "the mug with red hearts all over it." I remember that mug too, and how angry I was, but not what I was angry about, only the sad and confused look on Mark's face. I remember that I let it drop out of my hands onto the bathroom tiles, savoring the sensation of it smashing on the hard surface.

Depression is a horrible illness. At the height of it, or should I say the 'low' of it, I did all sorts of irrational things. One that I very much regret was that I went through the priceless storage boxes of my childhood memorabilia and threw a lot of it out. I loathed anything that was a memory of success. I can't remember how many things I threw away that day and in recent years I've looked for particular childhood items, only to find that they're gone forever.

My psychiatrist said that my obsessions would fade into the background once the depression lifted and I would be able to challenge my OCD thoughts more constructively. In the meantime, he suggested the following things which were a great lifeline to getting through this nightmare:

- Look at situations in perspective because risk is a part of all we do.
- Learn to recognize thought overreactions that turn everything into a catastrophe.
- Lead a normal life. Go to the usual places because avoiding them can make fears increase.
- Disperse anger by punching a pillow or other healthy ways of expending negative energy.

As the depression began to respond to medication, I prayed "The last two weeks I've increasingly felt like I've been sitting on the floor, steadily and hesitatingly putting a jigsaw together and someone keeps walking through it." As my depression was a side effect of the out of control OCD, I prayed "When fear becomes reality only in my mind and no one else's, how can it be explained? I hate where I am and my only hope is to have you cling to me as I alternatively brush you aside then call for you in the wilderness."

DEPRESSION AND THE CHRISTIAN

In *Luke's Journal*, 2002, the journal of the Christian Medical and Dental Fellowship of Australia, I was given a very helpful article 'Depression and the Christian[3]' by Dr Lachlan Dunjey. In this article, he gives a professional response to the questions that Christians often ask in relation to depression and Christianity. For a better picture of the terrible struggles that face those with depression, here is what he explained in a question and answer manner.

Q. "Surely spiritual people shouldn't get depressed?"

A. Christian people with high expectations of themselves may actually be more susceptible due to internal conflict. The Bible is very clear that we live in an imperfect world that is subject

3. Dunjey, "Depression and the Christian." 10–11.

Darkness (Having Depression)

to suffering and that all creation groans to be released. We all have vulnerabilities under stress, and depression from a medical point of view is no more of a failure than suffering any other disease process. However, some parts of the Christian community would regard any illness as indicating a lack of faith."

Q. "So being a 'good Christian' is not sufficient to maintain mental health?"

A. It is part of being a good Christian that while trusting in God we are to be personally responsible, to put faith into action to develop skills and strategies for ordinary living. For instance, to be a good and safe driver it is not sufficient to just be 'spiritual' but to develop skills in driving and to be personally responsible for such skilling. So, part of being a good Christian is to exercise Christian responsibility in taking care of our bodies and minds. This means when we are hungry we are to prepare food, and not just pray for manna. It means that when we are sick we commit our way to God, but also seek medical attention."

Q. "Why do depressed people feel failure?"

A. The loss of self-esteem and sense of failure that people feel in depression is intrinsic to depression . . . "

Q. "Surely guilt just requires getting right with God"

A. Guilt is an integral part of depression and is frequently worse in Christians. It is important to reassure Christians that when their sins have been confessed, that God *has* forgiven them, that their feelings of guilt are just a part of the depression and that the devil loves to accuse us. There is a great difference between God-given guilt related to specific events and the non-specific broad guilt of depression. Unfortunately, well-meaning Christians who say 'you need to get right with God' or 'you need to have more faith' sometimes aggravate this . . . "

Q. "Where does spiritual counselling come into all this?"

A. Spiritual counselling is integral, frequently not so much directed at the cause as at helping us to know the value of our resources which, in God, are vast. He knows and understands all about us, He comforts and invites and he is always with us, despite what it looks like. People of faith need reassurance that they have not failed God, that their depression is not their fault, that their guilt is a result of their depression, and that many people of faith have been likewise affected. We also need to understand that faith is not a guarantee that we will not suffer, but it is a guarantee that God is still with us, will bring us through, and will turn even this to good.

Dr Dunjey sums up his views in this way:

> Put simply, the message to the community is that depression:
> - Is common
> - Is not failure
> - Can occur no matter how intelligent and capable we are
> - Can occur in people of strong faith, presents in many ways and has many causes
> - Can be treated simply with a good outcome in the vast majority of cases
>
> Antidepressants are effective in restoring the chemistry and are not addictive

The challenge of ignorance and judgement from critical Christians

The great majority of reactions to my illness were kind and supportive, with many friends and family walking many miles with me as I recovered. I did, however, experience ignorance and judgement from practicing Christians on enough occasions for me to realize that mental illness has a long way to go to be de-stigmatized, especially in our churches.

Darkness (Having Depression)

The most gob smacking of these examples was at a home fellowship meeting one night, when I disclosed that I had experienced major depression and OCD. I quote the response of one committed Christian member of the group: *"Oh! But I thought you were a pillar of the church!"* She didn't come back to our group again and shortly after she left our church. I suspect my disclosure had come as a shock to her expectations.

Another friend asked me if I had prayed about my illness. Had I prayed about it? The question was loaded with assumptions; with which I am familiar. So which answer should I have given her out of my multiple choice list? I chose the one that went something like this: "I've prayed for healing many times, but instead of a miraculous disappearance of my illness, God is steadily healing me through medication and the help of my psychiatrist." And there ended that short conversation which was never resumed! Another group of Christian friends treated my news as if I hadn't said anything at all when I disclosed it during our brunch catchup. They went on to discuss someone else's workplace problems. Now that did hurt, but I have learned to 'guard my heart' as this book will reveal.

I used these experiences as an exercise in self-learning, forgiveness, humility and tolerance. I also learned to extend grace to others who just didn't know *what* to say at all when I presented them with my dramatic news. I never imagined that I would be in the place in which I found myself and so I can understand that they never thought I would end up in this situation.

I also ignorantly thought that as a practicing Christian I would have the resources to avoid a 'break down'. In the weeks leading up to my leaving work, I interpreted my anxieties as a big spiritual challenge in which I was failing and reasoned that I needed to try harder. This interpretation was a significant mistake. But in my desperation for an answer I attended a one-hour prayer ministry session through a healing prayer organization. This brought me temporary emotional and spiritual peace, but just two days' later I was very unwell again.

The Lava Tube

These reactions have spurred me on to write this book. My motivation for telling my story is found in this Bible verse from 2 Corinthians that sums it all up for me:

> Praise be to the God and Father of our Lord Jesus Christ, the Father of compassion and the God of all comfort, who comforts us in all our troubles, so that we can comfort those in any trouble with the comfort we ourselves have received from God. 2 Corinthians 1:3–4 New International Version (NIV)

My experiences of being judged and misunderstood were not unique. In order to find out if this problem was systemic across Christianity in Australia, I attended a Youth for Christ *'Cultivate'*-Training Seminar in 2009 called 'Depression and Anxiety', with the emphasis on youth. Those in attendance included counsellors, youth workers, youth leaders and pastors. For the lecture, guest speaker Lauren Thomas[4] produced the following list of attitudes and beliefs that she had professionally encountered:

- There must be something wrong with your spiritual life
- Real Christians don't get depressed
- You need to have more faith / Just have faith in God
- Taking antidepressants is playing God. He can heal you.
- Scripture says everything happens for your own good!
- You've been prayed for, why has nothing changed?
- Depression is a self-discipline problem
- You should be praying about this
- You just need to rebuke that spirit of depression
- It's not an illness, it's all in your mind
- You've got nothing to be sad about
- It's your own fault you're depressed

---

4. Thomas, "Anxiety and Depression." *Cultivate Training Session, Youth for Christ.*

- Pull yourself together
- Depressed people are just being lazy

The audience had the opportunity to give feedback on these attitudes and beliefs. Most of the group thought that these statements were unhelpful, brought shame and guilt and had been made from the perspective of ignorance, labelling those who don't meet their 'holiness bar'.

MY CAVE ANALOGY

In explaining to you of how I experienced OCD and depression I will share with you a poem that I wrote at the time of my breakdown about a walk in a cave during a bush walk that began pleasantly but went very wrong.

My cave analogy was inspired by a letter that Mark's parents had sent us. At the time they were on holidays in the Mt Eccles National Park in Australia's most extensive volcanic area in Victoria's western district and across the border into South Australia. They told us of long, narrow cave tunnels called 'lava tubes'. These captured my attention. I felt that they made an apt analogy for my recent experiences.

In order to understand my poem, it would be useful to explain how a lava tube is formed.

> Unlike most caves, which are formed by wind and water weathering and dissolving rock, this cave was once a river of lava! A stream of boiling lava flowed from the crater [of the now dormant volcano, Mt Eccles] and was quickly cooled by the air, forming a crust, but hot liquid lava continued to flow away beneath. Eventually the lava flows ceased, leaving a hollow tube.[5]

Here is an illustration by Oliver Rennert of the Undara Volcanic Park in Queensland, that helps explain.

---

5. Parks Victoria, "Mount Eccles National Park—Visitor Guide and Walks." 2.

The Lava Tube

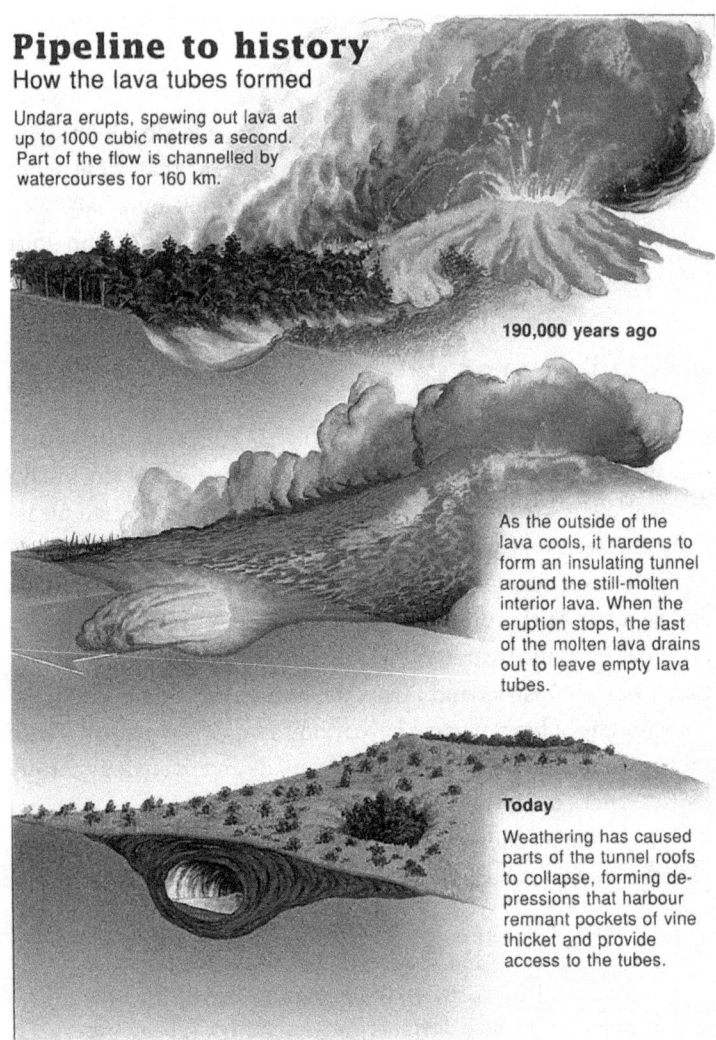

The Geological Process of How Lava Tubes Are Formed[6]

I was amazed that a quiet cave was created so tumultuously. I felt it symbolized what I had gone through in those early weeks after the 'breakdown'. I would put it in a poem. The poem was an

6. Oliver Rennert/Australian Geographic. Undara is a Volcanic Park in Queensland. Used with permission.

Darkness (Having Depression)

analogy of going on a bushwalk with friends, getting separated from them and lost in a volcanically active lava tube. While 'lost', it takes me a long time to realize that the fiery magma that I can see and feel in the cave, actually cooled down millennia ago. What I wanted to capture in words was:

- All-consuming anxiety catching and trapping me by surprise when I thought I could beat the fears in my head
- Energy-sapping depression
- God's rescue plan and the dawning realization and great relief that my fears were the result of illness
- The beginning of recovery

The Lava Tube

What was I looking at while my friends walked further down the track?
What preoccupied me so much to miss them moving on?
It's a bit embarrassing to have to catch up.
There's only one path to follow and it leads into a cave with damp ferns and emerald moss decorating its entrance.
I can feel the temperature drop as I hurry in—its damp chill is refreshing.

Further in I start to jog, stirring up the dirty floor into stale dust puffs with each stride.
If I were fitter I could jog faster, but I thought I was fit and ready for this hike.
I become nauseous with exertion but if I can keep jogging I know I'll catch up to them.

All of a sudden I can't see my feet, slam into a rock wall and land in the dust.
I hear staggered breathing and realize it's mine, echoing off the walls.

The Lava Tube

I'm lost.

The cave walls are glowing orange! There's lava here! The Bushwalking guidebook said nothing about this being an active volcano!
Immediately I'm overwhelmed with panic.
Ash is burning my scalp and blistering my hands.

I curl up like a millipede. Where did I go wrong?

Is that you, God? I am so ashamed for you to see me like this.
I push your reassuring hands away and try to think of what to do.

Time drags on but you're still here, kindly persistent, patiently compassionate.
I feel the brush of your fingertips and then a tug as they curl around mine.
I take your hand, stand up and start to look around.

I don't believe what I see-the stars are out!

No not stars—this place is full of glow worms!-Fragile, milky pearls sewn on a black stage curtain. Each one is a glimmer of hope.

A long way away I can see a way out and start walking up the slope towards it.
Although the path isn't steep, I slip and stumble much of the time but you catch me.

Finally, I am in the sunshine glare of outside.
Relief sends tremors through my body and my tears burn my eyes.
I stand on the edge of a great expanse full of afternoon color, shapes and light.

My fellow walkers are in view, smiling, chatting and munching on picnic sandwiches.

Darkness (Having Depression)

Looking back at the cave's exit, I recognize it from the guidebook.
It's a stone-cold lava tube.
Shuddering, I can still see the vile lava of fear superimposed on those beautiful glow worm walls.
With firmness I force myself to walk on.
My 'why's' and 'where did I go wrong's' must be left behind because there are few answers back there.

There's a new kind of peace in my mind.
One that is so new that it hasn't dried yet and I fear it will evaporate.
The smells on the breeze are exquisite, some sentimentally familiar, some new.
My trembling fingers are numb and tingling and I finally remember
that I'm still holding onto your hand, Father God—
But no! It's your strong grip that is still holding onto mine!

My slipping and tripping recovery to health

Now, as you've read, this poem has a happy ending. And indeed in an amusing postscript, God had more in store for me, to press home the point that he cares for me in every detail of my life!

Several years after writing this poem, we went on a family weekend to explore this amazing volcanic countryside because I wanted to see these lava tubes first hand. We had a wonderful time exploring Byaduk Caves that were formed from the volcanic flows of Mt Napier. The paths leading around the massive sinkholes felt hollow and bouncy beneath our feet. I called ahead to our children, then young teenagers, to be careful and I turned back to explore, for a second time that day, the entrance to Harman One Cave. It has a lush display of delicate ferns and plants like the ornate curtains of a nineteenth century musical theatre. It has a precarious entrance composed of a steep descent along a narrow slippery path lined with scraggy and fragile scoria rocks. My early healing process had seemed as insecure as the descent to this cave.

I paused for a concluding prayer of thanks to God for all that he had done for me over the seven years since my illness, and then began my climb back up the steps. Without warning I slipped! I just had time to call out instinctively "Mark!" (Who was 100 meters out of earshot!). I grabbed for but missed all of the sharp wet rocks that might have stopped my descent as I began sliding right back down to the cave! I landed on a ledge after slipping about a meter and I laughed hard spontaneously! God had indeed stopped me in my fall from being 'utterly cast down'!

I have included three photos of the area to help you visualize it, and three Bible references that talk about God's rescuing when we slip and slide in life's challenges.

There has been a lot of symbolic slipping and tripping in my management and recovery. It is a fact that I am grateful to state, that it is better to be here, at last understanding myself with the revelation of diagnosis than my life before. My perspective now is that I am grateful that I understand myself better, through the revelation of diagnosis of OCD rather than struggling on without the insights that diagnosis brings.

Even though the experience was very traumatic and losses have left their scars, I savor my life now. It sounds cliché but colors *are* richer, fragrances *more* stimulating and the simple things *more* delightful than before, when I didn't understand that OCD was the illness that plagued me since I was twelve.

Darkness (Having Depression)

Inside the Mt Eccles lava tube cave, taken in pitch black with camera flash (note lava flow ripples on the walls.)

My happy exit from the lava tube.

The Lava Tube

Byaduk Caves Harman 1-location of my slipping!

The Lord makes firm the steps of the one who delights in him; though he may stumble, he will not fall ("though he fall, he will not be utterly cast down" New King James Version), for the Lord upholds him with his hand. Psalm 37:23–24 NIV

Unless the LORD had given me help, I would soon have dwelt in the silence of death. When I said, "My foot is slipping," your love, O LORD, supported me. When anxiety was great within me, your consolation brought me joy. Psalm 94:17–19 NIV

I waited patiently for the LORD; he turned to me and heard my cry. He lifted me out of the slimy pit, out of the mud and mire; he set my feet on a rock and gave me a firm place to stand.
    He put a new song in my mouth, a hymn of praise to our God.
    Many will see and fear and put their trust in him. Psalm 40:1–3 NIV

4.

Dearest (My Family's Experiences)

OCD IS AN ANXIETY disorder that people do not easily understand. Its reputation as a peculiar illness involving compulsions of repeated checking and cleaning, makes it frequently the butt of jokes. It's also recently become a regular subject for voyeuristic TV docudramas and motion picture comedies. Although these shows can be funny, they gloss over the seriousness of the disorder, the despair of the sufferers and their families and friends. Through education about and acceptance of my OCD illness, I was able to retain insight into the condition. But quite often treatment progress can be a lot more difficult and even hindered for those who are conflicted by denial of their diagnosis or that of their loved one.

So far I have told you what a serious disruption OCD made to my professional and personal life, but what about those closest to me? How did my illness affect them? They have kindly given me permission to tell you about their experiences during this time. As you read on, please remember that OCD is a recognized and treatable illness. When my family and I gained an understanding of the mechanism of OCD, we began to gain the upper hand in managing it.

As explained in chapter 2, compulsions and obsessions can take up hours a day, with a flow on effect to families, friends and social interactions. Without an understanding of OCD, it's easy for family to get caught up in these rituals of behavior and requests for reassurance.

When I was first diagnosed it was hard for my immediate family to understand OCD. They had to learn what it was and eventually, how they could help me recover, alongside the efforts to recover that I was making myself. Understanding it *is* the key to recovery. I remember how confusing and disruptive the acute phase of my illness was for them. It changed the course of our lives in a direction I had never imagined. I was unable to work for more than 18 months, I could not return to my nursing career or the school and the children I loved nursing. For many months I became a mother obsessed and unreasonable about her children's safety. Our household income dropped dramatically and never returned to that of my professional nursing days.

Several years after the acute phase of my illness had resolved, I approached Mark and my children to give them the opportunity to share their experience of how this phase of my OCD experience affected their lives. I'm very grateful for their input, because they reveal valuable insights into the lives of family members of someone with OCD.

MARK

Until I was well enough to be self-sufficient again, Mark was my principal carer, though we never formalized the term. He was the one I leant on completely for support and reassurance. He alone withstood my uninhibited barrage of irrationality when I was drowning in the distress of intrusive, excessive fears. I unwittingly used him as a baffle against the dreaded chain of events I imagined.

A very strong theme was my *need for repeated reassurance*. I demanded Mark's full attention and responses with these compulsions. I would ask him up to five times to repeat his answer to my question "Did I lock the front door"? with very specific words such as "Yes, you locked the front door." A generalized answer was unacceptable to me because he had to follow the looping path of my thinking. I had to be sure that he hadn't misinterpreted my question. Sometimes after he had reinforced my need for reassurance multiple times, he would try to ignore me, or to make a joke, or change the subject, but these were all unsuccessful attempts at stopping my cycle of fear. I was never reassured.

Another ritual related to parking the family car. I would drag him into my demands to the point of exasperating him. When he was driving I would insist he park in the location that met my safety criteria, not his. Sometimes I would demand that he move the car if the spot wasn't 'safe enough'. In my mind it couldn't be parked anywhere where it could roll downhill and crash into a shop, house or intersection. It couldn't be parked where people would see me sitting in the car and come and talk to me. Sometimes it couldn't be parked anywhere, because nowhere suited all my criteria. If the car rolled away and injured someone, it would go against all that I stood for in being a model citizen. I would ruin everyone else's life, not just my own. How could my family live with my mistakes and irresponsibility? I would be on the verge of tears if it wasn't done *my* way or if Mark wouldn't move the car. I would be beside myself with worry until we returned to the car for me to see that indeed, it hadn't magically taken itself out of first gear, released its handbrake and gone somewhere by itself.

After my breakdown I put so many restrictions on our social life that it almost ceased. Mark could no longer invite friends over or stay after church for a cuppa and chat. He would have to make excuses for why I was absent from so many events. Socializing was always on my terms. I would list worst case scenarios for daily challenges that he couldn't have imagined in his wildest dreams and he would have to stop everything and address those challenges.

Mark's logical responses in the face of my obsessions did not work and if he showed his disappointment about my behavior in any way, I would implode with self-criticism and feelings of despair. He could not get me out of these behaviors by anything he said or did. It was very frustrating for him because he found it impossible to negotiate with me or rationalize me out of my worries and anxieties. My rituals were all illogical and he wasn't 'okay' with them, but he soon discovered that being critical of my behavior or trying to rationally change my mind was counterproductive. Mark summed this up: "I had to make it appear as if everything was okay when it wasn't. I was trying to keep the peace."

It was only when I was diagnosed that Mark could see that my thought processes were malfunctioning. He then felt empowered, slowly and carefully, to take firmer action with my behavior than he had before. He was compassionate in all his dealings with me because he could see it wasn't easy for me, but his frustration continued with my illogical thinking and unreasonable behavior. He clearly saw that my OCD was constraining all of us as a family.

Mark had to tread a delicate path between acceptance and response because he realized he could not change my behaviors and thinking by rational argument or disapproval. He saw that there was no point in him expressing any anger or frustration. He knew which behaviors were unreasonable and which were not, but only I could make the changes and I could not or was not doing that. *I* had to make the changes in my thinking and until I did we, as a family, were stuck.

Sometimes the path was emotionally precarious for us as I tried to keep moving towards recovery. Mark couldn't travel it for me, but sometimes he would push me just a little, as for example, when I wanted to rope him into an obsessive reassurance cycle. Having gauged if I had enough capacity to tackle a fear myself, he would say "No, I'm not talking about that" and leave me to deal with my obsession alone. I must say that this felt like trying to swim to shore alone out of a sea full of sharks, but, as I learned more about OCD's cycle of pathological doubt, I knew it was the right thing for him to do.

Pathological doubt

I'm hoping that by now that you have a clearer picture of life with OCD and the repercussions on those closest to us. This is why OCD is often referred to as *a disease of 'pathological doubt'*. Even though we all have doubts from time to time, this kind of doubt can't be rationalized. It can't be easily reassured and it can be relentless in undermining peace of mind.

For me, my pathological doubts went around in a vicious cycle. A cycle of trigger, doubt, worry, fear, obsession/compulsion, relief, vanishing relief, doubt, worry, fear, obsession/ compulsion, around and around again.

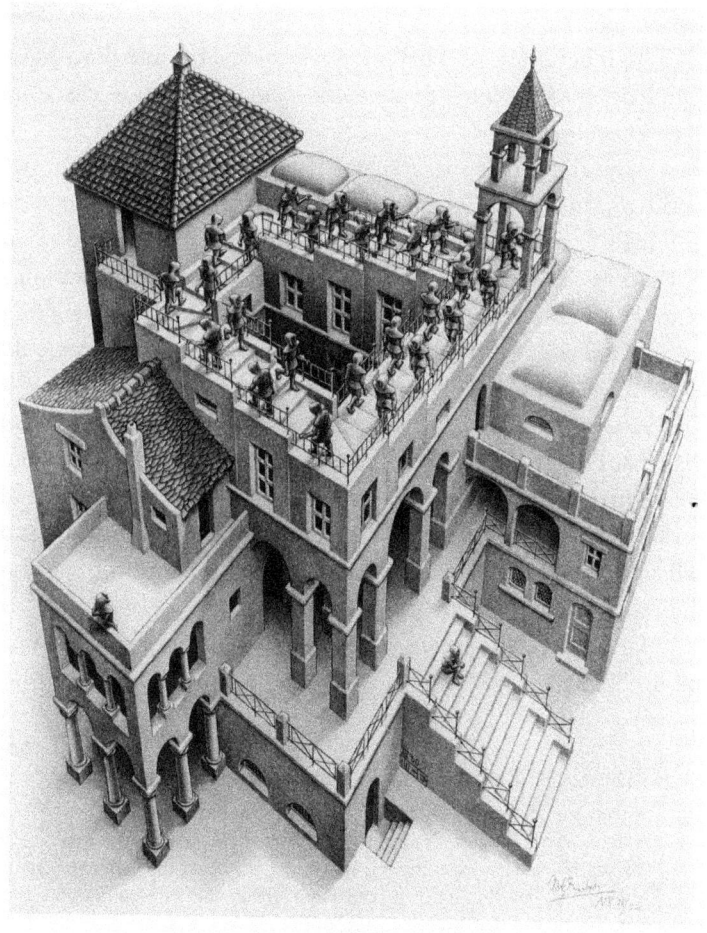

M.C.Escher's "Ascending and Descending"
© 2017 The M.C. Escher Company—The Netherlands. All rights reserved.
www.mcescher.com Used with permission.

The Lava Tube

This lithograph drawn in 1960 by Dutch graphic artist Mauritz Escher[1] is called 'Ascending and Descending'. Follow the steps of the soldiers as they go on their march around the top of their castle. At first glance the flight of stairs appears to lead them down, perhaps to the food hall to relax after their shift. But no! Now they're heading up again! They're caught in an endless cycle of going up and down, around and around. That's how obsessing felt for me.

To relieve my OCD pathological doubts, I would draw Mark into lengthy, convoluted requests for reassurance. Mark describes their effect on him:

"The thing that sticks in my mind as the most painful, repetitive scenario was when a simple decision degenerated into an argument, usually some simple little thing that we wanted to do but you would say no, for what appeared to me to be an irrational fear or unreasonable constraint. And that would degenerate into an avalanche of fears and eventually criticisms that you would express as being your fault with a fairly clear implication that it was actually my fault. What made these interactions so painful was that there were contributing circumstances on both sides but I couldn't argue the case because the conversation never stuck to rational paths. It got to the point where I couldn't say anything and whatever I said was wrong, so I would end up saying nothing and giving in to whatever you were on about."

Gradually I was able to articulate the thought processes going on inside my head.

---

1. Mauritz Cornelis Escher (1898—1972) was
    a truly unique artist whose vision was quite unlike anyone else's. To enter his world is to set foot into unknown territory. His extraordinary pictures of logic and perspective fool the brain into believing the impossible—that staircases can climb forever, that fish can morph into birds, and that water can run uphill . . . but it is his world of strange perspectives and distorted vision for which he will be best remembered. The fact that he was able to produce these visual conundrums again and again, delighted and mystified his public, many of whom were mathematicians.

Forty, Sandra, *M.C.Escher*, front inside dust cover notes.

Mark was then able to understand why certain things came out in certain ways and he could choose more systematically whether to engage with them or not. Irrational conversations were no longer senseless interactions between us. Now he was able to see more of the OCD patterns in my explanations and then he was able to pick and choose when to intervene.

FROM MY SON'S PERSPECTIVE

Now let me tell you how my son saw things through an eleven-year-old's eyes. His memories of this time were that I was highly strung and easily upset. He says:

"If I wanted to go on a bike ride, you wouldn't let me. If I was upset that you wouldn't let me go, you would turn it back on yourself and say that you had failed as a mother. Without explanation you would insist that I had to change something or get rid of something even though it seemed illogical to me. Was it just to annoy me or was it your overreaction? So I put it down to you being very strict. I stayed out of the way, invested my thoughts with out-of-home friendships and tried my hardest to please you. I didn't want to upset you or be another worry on your mind. The OCD episode went on for so long that it made our family more complicated."

His 11th birthday cake

One of the highlights of our children's birthdays was for me to bake them a themed cake of choice, such as Miss Piggy, Humphrey Bear, Humpty Dumpty or a racing car track. I had made this our very own family tradition and loved both the theme choices by our children each year, and the baking process. Four months after I left work, my son's eleventh birthday was steadily approaching. But I couldn't bring myself to bake his cake or to even have the party at our place—what if something happened to one of the children? What if they got gastroenteritis and died? Or hurt themselves playing in our yard? I'd never forgive myself and I'd be hated forever by everybody! This was a classic case of how my family was affected by my *thoughts and fears of contaminating foods* and *fear of causing harm*.

Unable to overcome these fears, I insisted that we went to a party venue instead (even though it blew the household budget). Instead of home baked goodies, I brought in take away food for them to eat. Instead of baking that special birthday cake, I had the cake made by the local cake shop. And instead of cutting and serving up that cake for the children and parents, I mumbled a lying, feeble excuse about how hopeless I was at cutting cake slices straight! When everyone survived the party and went home, I was exhausted and relieved. But I couldn't keep on buying birthday cakes and outsourcing celebrations for the rest of their childhood.

FROM MY DAUGHTER'S PERSPECTIVE

My daughter was eight when I was diagnosed. Her reflections about this time are equally insightful:

"Kids came up to me at school and asked "Why isn't your mum looking after us in our School Health Centre anymore?" but I didn't want to say and didn't understand what was wrong with you so I told them "Mum got bored."

I remember Dad trying to help me understand it, after you had shut yourself in your bedroom for a couple of hours. But I could tell that he was frightened and that made me really scared. Feeling Dad's shock from the whole thing impacted me as well. After that things started to settle down. But over the next couple of years I'd feel panicky that I might get OCD and get angry too like you did that time when you deliberately dropped a coffee cup on the bathroom floor. Dad always reassured me that the likelihood of me getting OCD wasn't very big.

There were moments that I got really frustrated with you when I had a normal request and you would say 'no'. When you were crying I would bring you a blanket. Sometimes I thought that

I could make things better—if I just did something it would all go away.

You would send notes to school for absolutely everything; like why I couldn't bring a library book to school, or had to wear non-uniform track pants, all the time. And that one time I came home and admitted to you that you didn't need to send notes all the time . . . it was getting embarrassing.

When you started taking the medication I thought "What on earth would they do? Why would she have to take those? How are they going to help? A pill can't help"!"

For my daughter to have a normal primary school experience and to be able to expect and rely on me to be a normal participating school mum, I knew that I needed to come to terms with my *avoidance* behavior and begin to visit the school regularly. The first time I returned it felt as stressful as an exam. Of course everything was completely normal when I went to the office, walked the corridor, chatted with staff and other mums. It was so very normal that I laughed when I got back into my car, then tears of relief mixed with regret sprang into my eyes. I felt relieved that I had conquered avoiding the school but regret that I could no longer work there with all the school children I had come to know, around 400 of them. I missed the rush of pride and love I that I used to feel when I worked there, when my own children popped their heads around the sick bay door to say hi to me, their mum.

'LAW AND DISORDER'

Let's take a look at the experiences of Ruth, another Christian with OCD. You might find it helpful to imagine yourself as her sister or brother, mother or father, or perhaps friend or colleague as you read her story. How would having your own basic understanding of OCD help you both?

In 2002, my parents read an article by Jess Stokes, in the Salvation Army's national weekly magazine *Warcry*. It told the story of lawyer Ruth Pollard, who shared her experiences of OCD. When I read Ruth's story I felt so comforted and encouraged. This was because I hadn't to date found many Christians willing to disclose that they had this disorder. I'm grateful for her honesty, courage and insights at that time. The following is quote from her story titled 'Law and Disorder'[2]:

> Not so long ago, an average day for Sydney lawyer Ruth would start at 5.00am, when she began her arduous ritual of showering, checking her skin for cancerous spots, and doing her makeup. This would usually take about three hours. Even so, Ruth never felt she had been thorough enough, but she also had a job to get to and needed to be on time to catch her bus. Yet even on the bus she would be gripped by two competing fears. The first was to do with germs and avoiding railings, door handles, seat covers—anything people had touched. The second, and much more consuming, was a religious compulsion to talk about God to whomever she was sitting next to. She felt utterly besieged by both compulsions . . .
>
> By the time Ruth's disorder was finally diagnosed, her condition had really escalated . . . Ruth explains. "Eventually I couldn't function on a day-to-day level. In the background there was always a terrible, terrible anxiety. It was constant. There was never any relief." While Ruth's condition could perhaps have been treated earlier, her religious obsessions made her reluctant to seek help, even when a doctor in the early 1990s recognized her symptoms and suggested she visit an OCD clinic. "I obsessed that by going to the clinic, I wasn't trusting God to heal, look after me, or even reveal what was happening in my life. The obsession was such that I thought wrong behavior was causing my torment and so the answer to the problem was prayer or seeking forgiveness rather than medical help. Of course, I know now that isn't the case. God wanted me to seek help."

HELPING THE CARER

The writer of Ecclesiastes says

2. Stokes, "Law and Disorder." 6–7.

Dearest (My Family's Experiences)

> Two are better than one, because they have a good return for their labor: If either of them falls down, one can help the other up. But pity anyone who falls and has no one to help them up. Ecclesiastes 4:9-10 NIV

So, what to do? These verses work both ways, in respect for an ill person and their friend. Who is there to support each of them?

Psychologist Kathryn I'Anson gives understanding and insights, suggestions and helping strategies for those who care for a person with OCD in her booklet . . . *nine, ten, do it again. A Guide to Obsessive Compulsive Disorder For people with OCD and their families*:

> If you are a spouse, sibling, mother, father, child or friend of a person who has OCD, then it is quite possible that you have been suffering too. Your worry, frustration and confusion arises from the impact of the OCD on your relationship and environment, and because it is so hard to see someone close to you battling and in despair over thoughts and behaviors that seem to make no sense. Maybe insidious guilt thoughts creep into your mind, "Is it my fault?", "What have I done wrong?", "Should I have loved and cared for him/her *more*?" Maybe you feel angry and confused—you simply can't understand how it is possible that this person, who seems quite rational in all other respects, just can't stop these ridiculous behaviors. Have you secretly wondered, "Is it attention seeking, laziness, naughtiness?" On top of all these conflicting feelings, there is the feeling of helplessness—you just don't know what to do.[3]

I'Anson goes on to say to the carer:

> The first thing to do is to find out enough about OCD so that you can let go of all these tangled and distressing feelings of guilt, blame, confusion and anger. You do not need to condemn yourself for having these feelings. They are natural reactions. OCD is quite alien to you—you do not understand it, know why it is there, or why it should affect this family member or friend. These feelings arise

---

3. I'Anson, Kathryn. . . . *nine, ten, do it again*, 6.

from ignorance and fear, and you will discover that there is no valid evidence to support them, and they are simply not helpful to yourself or the sufferer. The next thing to do is to realize that you can't effectively support and care for someone else unless you also have support and care.

There are national organizations and associations for relatives, friends and carers of the mentally ill that can assist in the education and support of carers. They can help make a real difference through support, education, conferences, information kits and help phone lines. Such organizations can help take the despair out of such situations families commonly find themselves in.

IN SUMMARY

The State Government of Victoria's Better Health Channel website provides health and medical information to help individuals and their communities improve their health and wellbeing. Here is what it says:

> It can be difficult, demanding and exhausting to live with a person who has OCD. Family members and friends may become deeply involved in the person's rituals and may have to assume responsibility and care for many daily activities that the person with OCD is unable to undertake. This can cause distress and disruption to all members of the family.[4]

As can happen, my OCD experience was a major disruption to my young family's life. But when we became enlightened about how it manifests, we gradually became more empowered to take away its power over our lives. ARC and organizations like it have excellent resources and I continue to be a member and receive their newsletters.

Over time, Mark and I learned that it would be detrimental to my recovery for him to suddenly stop the reassurances I sought

---

4. Better Health Channel, Obsessive Compulsive disorder—family and friends. lines 4–8.

when I was obsessing. But over time, he steadily reduced his level of involvement in them. To return to the cricket analogy, this meant that it was time for me to take my bat out to the pitch, set up my guard in front of the stumps and begin my innings in taking the offensive against OCD.

5.

Courage
(Developing Treatment Strategies)

THE FIRST FEW WEEKS following my abrupt departure from work slowly passed and gradually my depression diminished. It was time to take stronger measures to bring my OCD to a more manageable level. But how does one reinvent oneself after such an experience? I realized that what I'd been through in the last few months would strongly influence my future, so it was up to me to shape that future in as positive a way as possible by implementing the skills I was beginning to learn.

Many of these early days were still 'shaky days' when in the middle of a pleasant experience such as lunch with friends, I would unexpectedly remember an old obsession. 'Gollum' was still skulking around in my mind, upsetting my emotional equilibrium. The choice to opt out of actively participating in the world around me was frequently very appealing. In my anxiety, I suggested to myself that this would mean I would reduce the opportunities of making a mistake and therefore reduce the risk of having new worries to obsess about. Of course this was an unhelpful and unconstructive plan of action. In truth, I needed to make the effort to *increase* participation in the world around me. With little steps I needed to begin to take what my mind told me were 'risks' in my everyday life. That meant I would be taking the offensive on the path

Courage (Developing Treatment Strategies)

to functioning normally again. If I didn't, the Rosemary-imposed constraints on my world would trap me further and be harder to budge later on.

By now I hope that you have some understanding of OCD from my own personal story. In this chapter I want, as a layperson, to outline some of the various ways professionals seek to help people suffering from OCD and tell you how they helped me in my journey towards recovery. You will also see where my Christian spirituality played a useful part.

The treatment of OCD involves a range of strategies, and a multifaceted approach was what worked best for me. Hearteningly, research of OCD and refining of treatments continues to go on.

1. COGNITIVE BEHAVIORAL THERAPY AND BEHAVIORAL THERAPY

CBT is one of the significant keys to treatment and management of OCD. As the Anxiety Recovery Centre explains:

> Behavioral therapy can teach us how to decrease our compulsive behaviors through exposure to our fears. Being able to recognize that our anxiety will decrease and that the outcome of being exposed to something we fear will not be a disaster can help us to recover from OCD. In Cognitive Behavioral Therapy (CBT) we learn how our thoughts, feelings and actions are connected and how to deal with upsetting thoughts (obsessions) and feelings. The second part of this therapy involves training our minds to resist the OCD. Things like 'bossing back' and self-rewards can help us to respond in more positive ways to our fears.
>
> This takes time and needs an experienced therapist to help us retrain the way we react to things that make us worry. Support from family is a big help to us along the way to feeling more in control of our lives.[1]

---

1. Anxiety Recovery Centre, CBT and Behavioral Therapy. lines 1–6.

Obsessing and ruminating

Getting my thinking working better was a big part of my healing process. One of my thought process obsessions was with my facial expressions. Sometimes I would review, over and over, the facial expressions that I had used in recent conversations. (Sometimes I would even re-enact those expressions when I was alone—if I had ever been seen doing this, it would have looked quite silly). I would analyze them in case they could have been misinterpreted by the recipient. My fear was that I may have said words or made a facial expression or body language pose, that could have been taken as patronizing, uncaring or inattentive. On and on my thoughts would go. Sometimes I would even make a phone call to reassure people what I had meant when talking with them. But I also needed the reassurance that I hadn't caused offence.

This thought process is sometimes called rumination.

'Rumination' is a useful description of obsession and I was an expert at it. When cattle graze, they ruminate for eight to twelve hours. This process involves their food going back and forth i.e. regurgitating and re-eating, between the mouth and its four digestive compartments. There is a lot of belching and flatulence of the greenhouse gas methane that is produced by digestion-aiding bacteria. The docile cow lies down and enjoys the process. Rumination is an excellent digestive process for cows but not for human brains.

Courage (Developing Treatment Strategies)

My daughter kindly drew this dairy cow to simply illustrate how cows ruminate.

My ruminations were sometimes all consuming. I could barely wait to get away from a situation I was in, like church, coffee with a friend or for the family to leave for school and work, so that I could return to the OCD thought patterns of my mind. I aimed to sort it out, check it for any faults, to analyze, but ultimately to find relief. It had become an automatic process. When I remembered that I needed to pray about a simple matter, I'd tell God, "Just hang on a bit, I'll get back to you when I've figured all this out." When I was ruminating, I hated being interrupted and if I was, I would have to start all over again. It must have looked like I was day dreaming to those watching me. I became so tired, frustrated and worn out by all this mental work. A few times when daughter was talking to me I said to her, "Talk to me in a minute because I am 'thinking.'" I just *had* to say this because my drive to complete my rumination was overwhelming.

To help young people with OCD gain a better understanding, the Anxiety Recovery Centre Victoria produced 'A Guide for

Young People with Obsessive Compulsive Disorder"[2]. In it they explain the mechanism as to how obsessions often connect to compulsions.

> The more we try to stop thinking about something, the more we try to push a thought away, the more we end up thinking about it and the more intrusive the thought becomes . . . obsessional thinking is not silly, it is annoying, frustrating and upsetting. It almost makes us fear our own minds. Somehow, our talented mind becomes like a battleground . . .
> Compulsions are actions we take to try to *force* the threat from our minds. Generally, these actions (checking, cleaning, avoiding, asking to make sure) have to be done repeatedly, and sometimes in special patterns, until we feel some sense that the threat has been pushed away. The problem is, this only ever works for a short time, and before long the obsessive thought and doubt come back. So we start doing these repeated actions more often and more carefully, but the worry about the fear and the feeling of threat seem to get stronger . . . The repetitive actions, or compulsions, do not remove the threat, it just seems so because by repeating things 'well enough' or in the right way, we can feel we have done something about the threat. And maybe this time it will go away.

Every year I volunteered to be a backstage helper at C's annual dance concerts. The year of my diagnosis, I was standing side stage at the dress rehearsal with Angela, who was another mother and a good friend. As we stood there in the stage wings, I was ruminating over a recent scenario when I heard Angela saying "Rose . . . Rose!" She was looking at me, curiously. I was so completely absorbed in my rumination I simply hadn't heard her. I'd just phased right out of the conversation we had been having earlier. She was so kind when I explained that it was my worries creeping up on me. This was a wakeup call that I needed to continue to learn more about managing my thought processes. When I told my psychiatrist

---

2. l'Anson, Kathryn and Carne, Rod, *A Guide for Young People with Obsessive Compulsive Disorder*, 8–9,12.

about what had happened, he reassured me that it was indeed just another example of OCD rumination.

Distractions and rewards

An essential early part of my recovery was homework given to me by my psychiatrist, Dr F. He asked me to keep a chart and on this record my daily mood scale (best to worst), number of hours' sleep and comments. In the first three months my daily mood scale swung up and down so that my graph looked like a gradient profile from the Alps stages of the le Tour de France international bicycle race!

To reduce the distress of frequent panic attacks, Dr F suggested that I count red cars *en route* from A to B. Sometimes I had to do this out loud. On a few occasions the children joined in, but soon got tired of it. It took me a long time to tire of it and when I did, I switched to blue cars! It may be hard for you to imagine how anxiety can cause someone to need to go to such lengths during a suburban car trip. Other times I would distract myself by praying through the alphabet for others' needs. This was very satisfying and felt constructive.

In my homework journal, I was to write down triggers i.e. incidents, overreactions and emotions that I was experiencing and, when ready, challenge them using my personal capacity to see them in a balanced way. The strategy was to identify the obsessive thought and name it (Gollum) and then seek to avoid my thoughts going down the path of unhealthy obsessive logic, by distracting myself in one way or another. When I wasn't bothered by the trigger any more I could give myself a guilt-free reward. I had to have a list of distractions that worked and was not to sabotage these distractions with negative thinking. I kept a spiritual journal at the same time.

When it came to thinking negatively, I was quite adept. To counterweight those strong negative emotions, I needed to stockpile a list of pleasant memories and to walk myself through one of them. In this way I would be neutralizing the weight of unhealthy thoughts on my shoulders with healthy ones. At first it was difficult for me to come up with a pleasant list that I didn't immediately sabotage with negative thinking. By 'sabotaging' I mean I would search for any imperfection in it where I had been less than perfectly behaved, when I didn't please somebody or when I didn't measure up. Why was it so easy to accept other people's weaknesses and not my own? This is where perfectionism was such a bane. This is a prayer I wrote at that time:

> Dear Father, I have spent the last fortnight battling with the homework Dr F gave me. I find it so hard to find pleasant memories that don't immediately suggest some failure on my part. It is as if my brain can only see the one little black mark of a large and clean whiteboard.

I persevered in stockpiling several beautiful memories to draw on and walk myself through when distraction was needed. Here are some of them:

- Lying on my back in the middle of a New Zealand barley field trying to spot the skylarks singing in the clouds way above
- Watching ice crystals form on the inside of a bus window on the way to Mount Cook
- My surprise thirtieth birthday party at Sizzler Restaurant with family and friends
- As a child, finding dozens of scallop shells with my grandfather on Rosebud beach after a storm

The following are some examples from my personal journal as I continued to emerge from the 'cave experience'. You can see the progress of thoughts from unhealthy to more constructive through the following extracts from my homework and spiritual journals as I journeyed on:

- 18/4/2002. "4.45am. *It feels like the 100th time I've lined up for the start of the rest of my life, only to jump the gun and have to line up again. I fear I've failed at getting better and wasted time and been self-indulgent and cowardly. I've lost patience* with myself and despair at the bombardment of juggling balls I'm trying to keep in the air. So close to tears, so close to silly laughter, so close to progress, so frustrated by the delay. I want to say to people, 'I beat this Gollum'".

- 6/5/2002. "Day 3 of Resolution not to search for the failure in everything. The morning reminds me of driving to Uluru—dewy, quiet, starts with crystal sunrises, still air, anticipation. I'm desperate by afternoon to nap away the long hours. Escape memories, escape challenges, escape risk of participation, and escape the possibility of failure. The morning is full of anticipation. I have to go to do my volunteer morning. I don't want to go. Maybe I'll never want to go and commit to anything again. Later—glimmers of hope—a fun morning in the office. But glad to leave. I'm giving up and having a nap."

- 29/8/2002. "I've learned to find the joy in little things, not to overdo priorities that aren't important, the destructiveness of procrastination, to find pleasure in little goals, to accept my frailty, to accept little mistakes and accept other people's right to react and for me not to try to appease them."

- 14/10/2002. "What I long for is the ability to recognize healthy thoughts from unhealthy ones. I want to get over the pressure I feel, broaden my perspective, acknowledge undue need for reassurance and at the same time acknowledge my fragility. I want less stress headaches and chest tension, better endurance, to be able to smile at my mistakes, to be able to take risks at being honest and observing how others do it."

2. PRESCRIPTION MEDICATION

There are many prescription medications that assist in managing OCD and in conjunction with therapy can be very effective. In my case, medication made a huge positive difference in my life. Not everyone needs medication to manage OCD and many only need it for a short time.

Challenges

My medication, of the antidepressant variety, was the catalyst for my improvement. It lessened the effect of information that I would previously find anxiety-provoking. It made me less anxious and cleared my mind, allowing me to make decisions sensibly. It gave me room to stand up against my obsessions and compulsions.

At first finding the *right* medication and dose was quite a challenge. The medication I was first given was not specific enough to treat OCD and the second gave me a (rare) side effect. This side effect was 'expressive dysphasia', which meant that I began to get my words mixed up, not just occasionally, but regularly throughout the day. I would think one word but would say a completely unrelated one, or a scrambled one. It certainly was light entertainment for the family! Needless to say, I was swiftly taken off this tablet and commenced on the third medication which I was able to tolerate long term.

The following is a light-hearted poem I wrote spontaneously at the time, which gives testimony to what those early days were like when my concentration was poor and I couldn't rely on the words coming out of my mouth the way I planned.

I'm knitting a Computer

> *I wrote this little poem, I made it up myself,*
> *I thought of it just when I found my coffee on a shelf.*
> *I'd looked for it for ages,*
> *Perhaps a week or two*
> *And now its top is covered with a moldy sort of goo.*
>
> *'Forgetful' is the word for me as I head for the sink and*
> *Pour my coffee down the plug and have some time to think.*
> *The cup is really mucky, (The last one had dead flies)*
> *The stains I scrub remind me of the bags under my eyes.*
>
> *I'd lose on 'Wheel of Fortune',*

Courage (Developing Treatment Strategies)

They'd sound the losing hooter.
I'm knitting up a cardigan that I've called a computer.
My son is looking puzzled
And I am in a tizz –
Scientifically I'd told him that my underpants were his.

"Why did I come into this room?" It's a familiar scene.
Maybe I'll skip the decaf and head for the caffeine.
I thripped tree winners yesterday (tipped three winners) I say with pride and glee!
But my Footy Tipping's[3] *up the creek like a cat truck up a stree.*
(Cat stuck up a tree)

"I guess I really should slow down".
My family nod, relieved.
It's been a dizzy ride upon this carousel I'd conceived.
So soon I'll put my feet up and spray on some perfume and
Go and smell the roses
But first—
I need the broom.

You can see from my poem why the need to cease that second medication was obvious, and it needed to be done swiftly. I experienced some difficult symptoms during the changeover including emotional fragility, drowsiness and vision issues. For some days I could not drive. Another difficult factor was that the third type of medication, like the first two, took several weeks for me to feel any beneficial effect.

Establishing the best maintenance dose also took time. Once, after a trial on a reduced dose, I become cranky, irritable and overwhelmed. I was very disappointed that this meant that I needed to increase my dose again. I sought out one of our church leaders for

---

3. A footy tipping competition is held amongst a group of people e.g. a workplace or club, throughout a whole season of the Australian Football League. Weekly each person tries to predict (tip) the winners of upcoming matches. The eventual winner is the person who has the highest score for successful tips.

prayer about this. She said "Try to thank the Lord for every pill. See it as if taking medication is because you broke your leg again!" That was fantastically helpful and counteracted the *un*helpful expectations I had placed upon myself.

There have been phases when I struggled with the concept of taking medication, but I decided that for the sake of my family's wellbeing and my own, I would persevere.

3. ANXIETY MANAGEMENT

Keeping active

Exercise is also a useful part of recovering from anxiety. Thanks to modern science and its ability to discover what's good for us, we know conclusively that regular exercise helps with many illnesses. It helps to reduce stress and increase our metabolism, feeling a greater sense of well-being and personal satisfaction.

I was fortunate that, at that time, one of my sisters was a member of a weekly suburban walking club. She invited me to come along and try it out. I am forever grateful for her invitation and to the club for embracing me. Each week we would walk for an hour or more on walking tracks beside creeks and through valleys in our municipality. The pace that was set by the club was just right for me to feel that I'd 'blown the cobwebs away' from my muscles and my mind. At first I was nervous! I was by far the youngest of the walkers, not to mention slower than some of them twenty years older than me, but soon I stopped feeling self-conscious. I was there to enjoy myself and enjoy myself I did.

Each week I eagerly looked forward to the outing with my sister and the club, and after a while I felt confident enough to meet afterwards with the walkers for a cup of coffee and to join in the light-hearted conversation. Walking along bush tracks not only had the benefit of exercise but also got me out of my house where I would otherwise be spending my time laying on the couch and feeling obsessively fearful.

I recall Dr F saying that each day can bring its own uncertainties. So many things are out of our control which is tough for those with OCD whose major preoccupation revolves around avoiding hurting people. He explained to me that I needed to challenge these uncertainties and not avoid them. I should drive my car, meet with other people, go shopping and keep up my communal exercise regime.

On my own initiative, to meet his challenge in another way, I began a little portable veggie patch on our back veranda. I was encouraged to do this by my dear friend Jeanette who has a green thumb and had high hopes that I would grow one too! Watching little gourmet lettuces grow into something we could eat was a gentle and living reminder of hope for the future. Serving them up in a salad for my family was another little triumph over my compulsions related to food preparation.

Worry and stress management

Yet another way to deal with OCD is relaxation therapy. There is considerable evidence that relaxation therapy is a useful part of treatment of anxiety. Over the years I've had more than my fair share of stress-related medical problems. With the benefit of hindsight, I can see how these medical problems were the result of worry and stress that I had not dealt with.

In my twenties, I would get very anxious during social dinners. I would eat with a tense stomach. This precipitated painful indigestion, radiating from my stomach into my neck that would last for days. Once the chest pain from that indigestion was so strong that I went to Accident and Emergency, just in case it was my heart!

In my thirties I was plagued with headaches and migraines. I had a series of visits to a headache center where a neurologist coached me in a holistic approach to my problems. He identified my migraine triggers: what I ate, the amount of sleep I had, sun glare, cold wind and some perfume. As I worked on these aspects I improved dramatically. However, my tension-induced headaches remained. I hadn't been practicing the relaxation exercises that the neurologist had taught me. At my final visit he said "Rosemary! If you don't do your relaxation exercise homework, I'm going to send you to a psychologist!" Regrettably I continued to neglect this area.

In my forties and fifties, I clenched my teeth during my sleep so tightly that I developed a weak, clicking jaw joint—called 'Temporomandibular Disorder'. I put so much chronic strain on my jaw muscles that I reduced the distance my mouth could open to only two centimeters! At night I wear an acrylic splint that clips onto my lower teeth to reduce the biting pressure. This pressure can be up to ten times more than normal chewing in the daytime! I look like Bugs Bunny and sound like Elmer Fudd when I wear it, but it does help. Amongst those who can develop this disorder are singers and chronic worriers.

Now that my OCD had been diagnosed, I couldn't procrastinate any longer. I finally acknowledged that I must use some kind of relaxation technique as a permanent, smart health choice. I think I avoided this decision for so many decades because I had the false belief that my Christian faith was enough to keep my stress levels under control. Clearly it wasn't. I needed to learn, practise and implement the discipline of relaxation techniques to reduce my worry and stress levels, as a permanent lifestyle decision.

There are lots of different techniques to help us relax, including breathing techniques. Several of these techniques are portable and can be used 'on the spot' when needed or regularly during the day. Another relaxation therapy that has become popular in recent years is mindfulness. Simply put, it is calmly observing what you are physically feeling and thinking during a present moment.

Another path is Christian meditative prayer. When my parents were in their early retirement years they were introduced to this by their parish priest. They became members of the Australian Christian Meditation Community, part of The World Community for Christian Meditation (WCMM). By learning and refining this practice using a mantra such as "Maranatha, come Lord Jesus", they were able to still but not empty their minds, It allowed God to do his work in them. They felt more settled, at ease with the world and experienced the slow healing benefits of the spiritual insights they received through what became a life-long practice.

They lent me some of their resources to explore myself and I found them helpful. So much so that in the future I would like to study the art of Christian Contemplative Practice.

Biblical imagery—deep roots

Through the turbulent early months after my OCD diagnosis, I recognized that I needed to establish both mental and spiritual 'deep roots'. Roots that would grow wide and deep enough to stabilize me in times of stress and anxiety. And roots that would tap down to deep life-giving water courses during a parched spiritual season.

Whilst thinking and praying about this, the image of a large river gum emerged. Even in prolonged Australian drought, the river red gum does not easily die. The river red gum can live up to a thousand years! It can also survive long periods of inundation because floods are part of its cycle. I needed to be like a river gum with my strategies for managing OCD firmly established. I can't survive on 'just one drop' of water, trying to be wise and having my act together. I need to be permanently located 'beside the river'; with my roots drawing up the resources I have found to flourish. It was relaxing and reassuring to ponder regularly upon that tree. As Jeremiah said:

> But blessed is the man who trusts in the LORD, whose confidence is in him.
> He will be like a tree planted by the water that sends out its roots by the stream. It does not fear when heat comes; its leaves are always green. It has no worries in a year of drought and never fails to bear fruit. Jeremiah 17:7-8 NIV

In search of these magnificent trees Mark and I enjoyed an exploration of the Tahbilk Lagoon on the historic Tahbilk Winery Estate, Nagambie (established in 1860), beside the Goulburn River

Victoria, home of a lovely river red gum forest. There the gums grow solid and magnificent.

**River Red Gums at Tahbilk Lagoon on the Goulburn River.
Taken with permission.**

Indeed, as Proverbs says,

> Hope deferred makes the heart sick, but a longing fulfilled is a tree of life. Proverbs 13:12 NIV

Courage trees

Sometimes, despite strong growth, trees can be blown over by a storm. But even when they are lying on their side, some of these trees have such deep roots they can survive. The branches that were not crushed in the fall then grow from the trunk upwards to the sky like a new row of saplings. I call these trees 'courage trees' because despite their trauma, they persevere. They remind me of this verse:

> Have I not commanded you? Be strong and courageous! Do not be terrified or dismayed (intimidated), for the Lord your God is with you wherever you go." Joshua 1:9 the Amplified Bible

A "courage tree" at Tahbilk Lagoon on the Goulburn River.
Taken with permission.

Music and the sounds of nature

Music has always been a huge part of my life. In the 1970s my father was a member of the World Record Club and would regularly bring home marvelous vinyl albums that would fill the house with the classics of European and English orchestral music of past centuries. Throughout high school my love for music was nurtured and continues on to this day. Due to this blessing I had an endless supply of poignant, positive songs or melodies that I would immerse myself in, even if only for a few minutes' peace. One in particular is *Deep Peace*, originally a traditional Gaelic blessing, arranged by Canadian songwriter Bill Douglas as a serene choral version. Here are the lyrics:

Deep Peace

> *Deep peace of a running wave to you*
> *Deep peace of the flowing air to you*
> *Deep peace of the quiet earth to you*
> *Deep peace of the shining stars to you*
> *Deep peace of the gentle night to you*
> *Moon and stars pour their healing light on you*
> *Deep peace to you*

Another effective way for me to relax was nature CD recordings that are restful to listen to. Whether it be wind in desert sheoaks, waves lapping in rock pools, or a chorus of frogs in a muddy dam, they are all appealing! I now absolutely love and regularly explore nature settings.

4. EDUCATION

Getting to understand OCD is another very important factor in the healing process. The last significant strategy that was used in my early management was education. Initially this meant gaining an understanding of OCD and its management from reputable sources. Dr F recommended that I consider joining the Anxiety Recovery Centre to receive their quarterly magazine and to have access to their other publications. He also suggested that I read Jeffrey Schwartz' book *'Brain Lock'*. It is a self-treatment method to 'free yourself from obsessive compulsive behavior'. However, as there are always risks involved in utilizing self-help books without professional guidance, some caution is needed in relying too much on such books.

Nevertheless, self-help books can teach us very richly. One day when I was feeling flat and despondent I decided to get out of the house and drive for half an hour to Tooradin Village beside Western Port Bay in Victoria. Sitting on a park bench at Sawtell's Inlet, I began to read Schwartz' book. Occasionally I looked up to watch a school excursion explore the low tide mud flats. But soon I was engrossed in *Brain Lock* and found myself reading it like it was a best-seller. I will never forget reading in it the recounting of the OCD experience of 'Roberta'. A pelican could have sat beside me and I wouldn't have noticed! Schwartz related Roberta's story as follows:

> Roberta would drive over a bump or a pothole and suddenly panic, imagining that she'd hit someone.[4]

Roberta would then double back to check if she had indeed run over someone. I was astonished—this was exactly what *I* did! No one told me to do it, I hadn't seen anyone else do it nor had I ever read about this kind of behavior. But there it was in print! To me this was a revelation as clear as an X ray confirms a broken leg. Suddenly I didn't feel so alone. There were other people in the world suffering and trying to regain control of their lives, just like me!

VOLUNTEERING

Getting involved in life outside of the home is hugely important in beating OCD. Many months after my diagnosis, I began to grow restless from the lack of a job but I certainly was not ready for a paid position. Dr F suggested I might like to try a volunteering role, so I went to a local City Council's Volunteering Information session. My energy levels were still quite low and my self-esteem

---

4. Schwartz, *Brain Lock*, xxviii.

was in tatters, but I began volunteering one morning a week at a women's center run by the Presentation Sisters of Victoria.

The center, "Wellsprings for Women" is a most beautiful haven in the busy municipality of Dandenong. It welcomes women from all cultures, faith backgrounds and abilities and was firmly committed to the principles of social justice, particularly for women of refugee or migrant background. My role was as an office helper; answering the phone, welcoming visitors, keeping the roll for the morning's activities and collection of the small attendance fee. Here I felt anonymous but useful. No questions were asked about my background. No one knew my story and I liked it that way. The Sisters were marvelous in their servanthood and always encouraging to the quiet volunteer who struggled with even the responsibility of collecting those small fees from clients each week. That volunteer was me.[5]

Slowly, with these management strategies now part of my daily life, I began to really embrace the fact that OCD was something that I had, not who I was. I was moving into a new phase where stability had returned and with it a new variety of challenges to meet.

---

5. Wellsprings for Women was founded by active community member, Sister Ann Halpin (1939–2009) after whom Halpin Way, Dandenong is named. Referred to with permission.

6.

Pearls (My Long Term Recovery Management)

MORE THAN TWO YEARS had gone by since my diagnosis. Now that my previous pathological fears had dissipated, peace of mind was a much more familiar emotion for me and I began to bask in the bliss of relief. Instead of curling up in distress when trying to fall asleep, I would doze off with my arms over my head, like a lolling cat stretched out on its back, absorbing solar energy from the afternoon sun! Cats only sleep in this position when they feel absolutely safe.

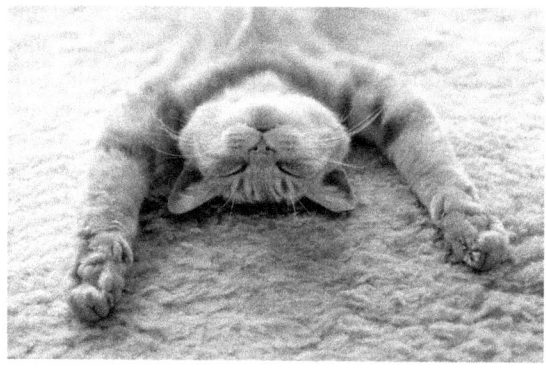

A peaceful doze![1]

1. Michele and Tom Grimm/Alamy Stock Photo G3RRWC. Used with permission.

I had progressed to a much better stage of stability along my path to recovery. But I still needed to make important positive changes to many unhelpfully engrained thought processes in order to help sustain my recovery in the long-term. These changes were not as much about specific strategies to manage OCD, but more holistic attitudes to embrace and practical steps to take. I needed to:

- address my struggle with perfectionism and fear of failure
- come to a point of acceptance of my OCD long-term
- put in place holistic strategies of self-care
- recognize my triggers for anxiety and
- rehabilitate back into the workforce with a new career direction

As I said in chapter 2, I wanted a cure for my OCD. I wanted to be a different person. More than once since diagnosis, I had responded to an altar call for prayer in church services for divine healing from my OCD. But that didn't happen. For most people it doesn't. Now I was finally ready to learn about becoming a healthier, functioning 'me'.

Recapping on my aims, I'd like to repeat the Anxiety Recovery Centre Vic's definition of 'recovery' that I referred to in that chapter;

> Recovery involves gaining quality of life through meaningful roles, relationships, and participation in the community. Recovery is less about cure and more about living a satisfying life. There will inevitably be times throughout recovery when your progress dips, or even regresses. Relapses are a part of recovery, and instead of viewing these backward steps as a 'failure', it is important to recognize them as an opportunity to learn about yourself. By doing this you can effectively determine your triggers in order to better handle future situations.
>
> Just as living with anxiety is an individual experience, the process of recovery means different things to different people. While you may not return to full health, you will gain an ability to manage symptoms so that they do not interfere with everyday activities.[2]

2. Anxiety Recovery Centre, What is recovery?. lines 1–10.

… PEARLS (MY LONG TERM RECOVERY MANAGEMENT)

ADDRESSING MY STRUGGLE WITH PERFECTIONISM AND FEAR OF FAILURE

Not everything I was thinking could be attributed to OCD alone. Since childhood I had developed very unhelpful personal expectations that now needed to be addressed. These had had a seriously detrimental effect on my self-esteem. My Christian faith remained strong, but my self-esteem was rock bottom. Perfectionism and fear of failure were the root causes.

I was prone to excessive self-evaluation. I would enjoy an experience but then spoil my enjoyment afterwards by automatically analyzing it for imperfections. I felt guilty that I was not perfect! Even though I knew it was absolutely valid for everyone else to make mistakes, I also believed it was not valid for me. I would be in turmoil for days thinking, "You aren't allowed to enjoy yourself! You don't deserve to enjoy your day! Look at all the mistakes you've made in your life." This drained the zest out of many activities that should have been a delight to be involved in.

Failure. When you're just not good enough!

It was hard for me to accept failure, especially when I had become obsessed about failing and knew that failure is part of living.

I had a significant breakthrough from 'out of left field'. It was in the form of the following incident that reawakened my lost sense of humor, made me chuckle at myself and still does! This particular day I was searching the internet for a 'motivational' poster for a friend. At this time motivational posters had become a huge craze. They were hung from board rooms to gyms, printed with inspiring attitudes and phrases like Dream Big, Be Courageous, Use Teamwork, Take up the Challenge and The Path of Integrity.

As I scrolled through the Internet I came across a group of funny posters that were aptly described as 'demotivational'! Intrigued, I looked at the collection and amongst them was a silhouetted bear cub trudging on its two feet into the sunset, with a caption "Failure: when you're just not good enough"[3]. Its stooped shoulders and lowered head were so much like human dejection! It so captured the disappointment of failure in such a humorous way! It was so opposite to the myriad of motivational posters, I had to laugh! A little like this bear cub (figure 11) who looks somewhat embarrassed at being seen, losing its balance!

Brown bear cub loses its balance![4]

I realized that I'd been taking myself far too seriously. I needed to accept that there wouldn't be a day when I would be perfect and

3. The original image described was photographed by Kitchin & Hurst/Kimballstock, called "Silhouette of Grizzly Bear Cub Walking On Hind Legs Sunset Rocky Mountains and the poster subtitle "Failure, when you're just not good enough" was produced by Pyramid Posters Leicester UK.

4. Cultura Creative (RF)/Alamy Stock Photo E8AR39. Used with permission.

could then resume my previous life. I was not the one exception to the rule of humanity's imperfections. Jesus was! This kind of thinking was completely at odds with his teachings. There would *always* be challenging circumstances to deal with and I had to take risks just like everyone else. The following poem that I heard at an ARC Victoria Conference, sums it up.

Risk

> *To laugh is to risk appearing a fool,*
> *To weep is to risk appearing sentimental.*
> *To reach out to another is to risk involvement,*
> *To expose feelings is to risk exposing your true self.*
> *To place your ideas and dreams before a crowd is to risk their loss.*
> *To love is to risk not being loved in return,*
> *To live is to risk dying,*
> *To hope is to risk despair,*
> *To try is to risk failure.*
>
> *But risks must be taken because the greatest hazard in life is to risk nothing.*
> *The person who risks nothing, does nothing, has nothing, is nothing.*
> *He may avoid suffering and sorrow,*
> *But he cannot learn, feel, change, grow or live.*
> *Chained by his servitude he is a slave who has forfeited all freedom.*
> *Only a person who risks is free.*
>
> ANONYMOUS

FURTHER CBT

During this time Dr F suggested I consult a psychologist who specialized in Cognitive Behavioral Therapy, in order to gain further skills in challenging my unhelpful thought processes and replacing them with healthier ones.

Over five consultations with that psychologist, I produced these statements that became new foundations for my healthier thought processes;

- I don't like having OCD, but it is not constructive to denigrate myself with unrealistically high standards of how I should think, act and live
- I need to accept that OCD is my 'cross in life'
- I'm doing the best under the circumstances
- I am a person of worth
- I'm just as valuable as anyone else, no matter what
- Some of my thoughts are 'nutty' thoughts—so what?! They are part of what makes me creative. I need to accept them and not fight them
- I need to accept myself and others as they are.

The most significant of these statements for me was, "I don't like having OCD, but it is not constructive to denigrate myself with unrealistically high standards of how I should think, act and live." Even with all the insight I had gained, I was still condemning myself for my OCD. That *had* to stop. And it did. With deliberate attitude change, I began to like being 'free to be me', to make mistakes, get embarrassed, be gullible and laugh at myself. In fact, I think I became more playful and light hearted. I had filled a river bed with my tears and now it was time to mop up. Today my perfectionist trait is just a faded memory without an emotional connection to who I've become.

In working at changing my unhealthy mind sets, there *were* failures and successes. From time to time I needed to rest and refresh, and have plenty of pep talks from my husband, sisters, friends and Father God through his Word, to keep me fighting for recovery. Sarah Groves, a gritty contemporary Christian singer/

Pearls (My Long Term Recovery Management)

songwriter wrote *The Boxer* in 2004. I love these lyrics because they draw an analogy between the Christian life and a boxing match. They remind me of the fight with OCD that was in my hands and the challenges of taking the offensive against it.

The Boxer[5]

> When you said this was a fight, you weren't kidding
> When you said this was a fight, you were not kidding, kidding
> Cause my ribs are bruised and it's just round two
>
> When you said this was a fight, you weren't kidding
> When you said this was a fight, you weren't kidding
> Cause there's a cut on my eye and it's just round five
>
> And I used to be quick I used to see it coming
> I used to know how to move my feet
> Now I can't duck and I can't land nothing
> And I forgot how to bob and weave
> Bob and weave
>
> When you said this was a fight, you weren't kidding
> When you said this was a fight, you weren't kidding, kidding, kidding
> Cause this room's in a spin and it's just round ten
>
> If you care at all take that towel from your neck
> Cause I've reached down deep and there is nothing left
> I've got nothing
> I've got nothing
> I've got nothing
>
> And I was talking big
> I was talking, but now, now what

---

5. THE BOXER (Sarah Groves) © Sarah Groves Music. Used with permission.

> *Greater is he who is in me*
> *Greater is he who is in me*
> *Okay, okay*
> *Greater, greater*
> *Greater, greater*
>
> *Bob and weave*
> *Bob and weave*
> *Bob and weave*
>
> *And I can't just know it, I've got to feel it*
> *And I can't just feel it, I've got to believe it*
> *And I can't just believe it, I've got to live it*
> *And I can't just live it.*

COMING TO A POINT OF ACCEPTANCE OF MY OCD LONG-TERM

I realized it was time to accept what had taken place in my life and move on. This process took several years! It was a long hard journey to learn to think in healthier ways. During one of my regular visits to Dr F, I was feeling sorry for myself, thinking that no one would ever value me again. "Who would want to spend time with or find value in someone like me, whose brain doesn't work properly"? He wisely replied that it's okay to like an old comfy chair rather than a new one. Many people prefer the comfort of an antique with its scratches and worn parts rather than a new piece of furniture—"furniture that has a story behind it." As time passed, I did come to like who I had become; a person with her own special story despite the dents and scratches.

The fact that I was struggling with a complicated and misunderstood anxiety disorder no longer undermined who I was in Christ. Did this acceptance happen overnight? Absolutely not! But giving myself permission to have this condition was the liberation I needed. Breaking the self-condemnation cycle is essential to self-acceptance. And self-acceptance frees us to be ourselves, to make mistakes, to be embarrassed, to learn, to be silly, laugh at ourselves and grow.

PUT IN PLACE HOLISTIC STRATEGIES OF SELF-CARE

As I continued to implement and refine my treatment strategies, I supplemented these with my own self-care. For me this meant stockpiling inspiring quotes, Bible verses, songs and stories that became precious pearls of wisdom for me. I could then draw on them when I was emotionally challenged. The following describes a few of those 'pearls' that were and still are significant for me.

'Knowledge is power'

This quote has been attributed to Sir Francis Bacon[6], an English philosopher who lived 500 years ago. I heard it an ARC Victoria 2002 Seminar for OCD & Anxieties Disorders Week.

Knowledge can promote new understanding. Understanding OCD can be a revelation for the sufferer and a significant key to management. As I've said previously, when I became better educated about the mechanisms of OCD, this quote became useful for me. I was no longer in the lava tube of confusion. I could see the path out. I firmly believe too that the more I knew about this illness, the more insight I gained. The more alert I was to its wiles, the more equipped I was to recover.

Sir Francis Bacon was a devout Christian. It's said that he may have been summing up two verses from the Book of Proverbs:

> The wise prevail through great power, and those who have knowledge muster their strength. Surely you need

---

6. Sir Francis Bacon (1561—1626) was an English author, courtier, & philosopher who wrote this phrase in his book Meditations Sacrae and Human Philosophy.

> guidance to wage war, and victory is won through many advisers. Proverbs 24:5–6 NIV

Knowledge is indeed power. In that newly found knowledge, not only did I find my own liberation and self-acceptance but suddenly I was more compassionate of others' mental illness struggles. It became a poignant feeling to have the revelation of a little understanding and insight into the plight of those much sicker than me. I was now able to feel *real* empathy for them in their challenges. I now understood first-hand how fragile and vulnerable the human mind can be.

'A precious flame'

Compelled by this new insight, I decided to hear a professional perspective by attending our regional public hospital's lecture series on 'Spirituality and Mental Health' presented by the Mental Health Chaplaincy and Pastoral Care Team. Twenty years earlier my general nurse training had only covered the basics of mental illness and provided just a four-week work placement at a private psychiatric hospital.

At the lecture, pastoral care for those with mental illness was elaborated upon. The possible origins and current causes of stigma towards mental illness were listed. A synonym for stigma is 'disgrace' i.e. 'without grace'. Unfortunately, ignorance and fear can cause those with severe mental illness, such as schizophrenia and bi-polar disorder, to be treated without grace. Patients can be labelled and pigeon-holed by their diagnosis.

The following quote appeared on the lecture series pamphlet that was distributed for the day. It is by PhD Psychologist Patricia Deegan's article "Recovering Our Sense of Value after Being Labelled Mentally Ill". I found it touching, insightful and inspiring:

> You may have been diagnosed with a mental illness, but you are not an illness. You are a human being whose life is precious and is of infinite value. You are precious and good. You are not trash to be discarded or a broken

object that must be fixed. You are not insane. You do not belong in institutions for the rest of your life. You don't belong on the streets. You are a human being. You carry within you a precious flame, a spark of the divine. You were born to love and to be loved. That's your birthright. Mental illness cannot take that from you. Nobody can take that from you.[7]

'Guard your heart for it is the wellspring of life'

Another pearl that I placed in my stockpile was Luke 10:27. God designed us with the four facets; heart (our spirit), mind (our thinking), soul (our emotions) and strength (our physical body). We're wonderfully made![8] After all, when being quizzed by a Pharisee about eternal life, Jesus answered,

> "'Love the Lord your God with all your heart and with all your soul and with all your strength and with all your mind', and, 'Love your neighbor as yourself.'" Luke 10:27 NIV

Any, some, or all of these parts can get sick. When a Christian's body gets sick, there is usually no issue, but I hope you now recognize that there can be a lot of stigma attached to the situation when the Christian's mind gets sick. And oh how easily the heart and soul are weighed down when the mind is unwell! It's because these four facets of our humanity are so interconnected.

This leads me to my next pearl. It's found in another Bible passage, this time from Proverbs Chapter 4.

> Pay attention to what I say; listen closely to my words. Do not let them out of your sight, keep them within your heart; for they are life to those who find them and health

---

7. Deegan, "Recovering Our Sense of Value after Being Labelled Mentally Ill." 7–11. Used with permission.
8. In reference to
   Psalm 139:14 NIV—"I praise you because I am fearfully and wonderfully made; your works are wonderful, I know that full well."

to a man's whole body. Above all else, guard your heart, for it is the wellspring of life. Proverbs 4:20-23 NIV

The NIV Study Bible describes health in these verses as "physical, psychological and spiritual."[9] It's another version of Luke 10:27. We need to watch over our heart (spirit) most intently of all. From this insight, I discovered that I could use this phrase as a 'health checklist' for when I needed to identify if I was under too much unhelpful pressure, whether internal or external in origin. 'Guarding my heart' was an initiative I could take during the ups and downs of life's challenges that could exacerbate my OCD. Guarding my heart was to give its health high priority.

'Emerging inch by inch'

My last pearl of wisdom was a compilation of songs that I could play any time I needed relaxation, reassurance or inspiration. These were the songs that I had discovered during my acute phase of illness. Whether they were a soothing blessing like *Deep Peace* or a challenge to persevere, like *The Boxer*, they all had their special place in helping me. In order for me to have them at my fingertips whenever I needed to hear them, a friend put them on a CD for my personal use. I called this CD 'Emerging Inch by Inch'. That title was to remind me how I'd emerged slowly but surely, alive from the lava tube.

RECOGNIZING TRIGGERS FOR ANXIETY

In respect to long term management, I also needed to learn to identify any triggers that might predispose me to regressing or even relapsing back into acute OCD. By learning to identify these triggers early, it was hoped that I could avoid getting as sick as I had the first time.

9. Barker, Burdick, Stek, Wessel and Youngblood, "The NIV Study Bible," 951.

Pearls (My Long Term Recovery Management)

Over the years, I learned to recognize if my thoughts and behaviors were developing into obsessions or compulsions. I also learned what the triggers for setting them off were. Often it was when I'd taken on too much responsibility or was putting myself under perfectionist pressure in certain situations. Other triggers were when life events were very challenging and out of my control.

I would then visit my local doctor to discuss what I was experiencing and together we would come up with an action plan to manage the situation.

Worms!

Inchworm, sketched by my daughter, 2008

THE LAVA TUBE

A local inchworm (also called a "Looper")[10]

A few years after my breakdown, I heard a favorite childhood song of mine on the radio. It was the witty actor Danny Kaye singing *Inch Worm*[11] from *Hans Christian Andersen*, the 1952 Hollywood Musical film. It describes a little inch worm that only has legs at both ends of its body, not along its body length. By drawing up its body into an arch to move along, the Inch Worm gives the impression that it is measuring wherever it is going. Even its formal name, the Geometer moth, means 'earth measurer'. In the song, Songwriter Frank Loesser describes this methodical worm

10. family *Geometridae*, photo by Mark (2015).

11. THE INCH WORM. Words and Music by Frank Loesser © copyright Frank Music Corp. Used with permission.

as so absorbed in 'measuring' a radiant flower that it misses out completely on enjoying the flower's beauty. Here are his lyrics:

The Inch Worm

> *Two and two are four*
> *Four and four are eight*
> *Eight and eight are sixteen*
> *Sixteen and sixteen are thirty-two*
> *Inchworm, inchworm*
> *Measuring the marigolds*
> *You and your arithmetic*
> *You'll probably go far*
> *Inchworm, inchworm*
> *Measuring the marigolds*
> *Seems to me you'd stop and see*
> *How beautiful they are*

Why was this song important to me? It was because I used it as a prompt to gauge whether I was obsessing over something rather than enjoying it. If this was the case, then I'd possibly be missing out on something special. There were delights of life and friendships God had put right in front of me, like the marigold under that inchworm, that I would miss out on if I was obsessing about something.

REHABILITATION BACK INTO THE WORKFORCE AND A NEW CAREER DIRECTION

Even though I was still deeply humiliated by the whole experience that I'd been through, I now knew that I could go on. I could be a woman who although she had 'broken', could still live a full and whole life. My nursing career was the greatest casualty of this whole experience. I couldn't return to my nursing profession. I was not willing to put myself back under the demands that a nursing career requires.

I wanted to return to the workforce but if I was to retrain in some other career I needed to be well before I could take on such a challenge. I was referred to a case manager with the Commonwealth Rehabilitation Service. She enrolled me in a 'Take Charge of Your Life' course at the local neighborhood center. I attended the course every Wednesday for five months. It was comprised of a skilled facilitator leading a small group of women who had each had their own life crises and even tragedies. Together we explored life skills that would build up our self-esteem, help us in communication, lessen guilt and stress, and strategies in avoiding or handling conflict effectively.

During this time, I was invited by a friend to assist her with her job during the busy Christmas retail season. She was a visual merchandiser with a large linen and bedding company with 13 retail stores across Melbourne. I was *very* apprehensive and lacking in self-confidence but I decided to take up her invitation. I'm so glad I did! My job was to work as a temporary employee, assisting her to produce displays of beautiful bedding, Christmas napery and decorations.

You may be wondering how I coped with return to the workforce and my ongoing OCD. There were times when I worried about the possibility that my displays on high shelves would fall down, landing on someone's head, even killing them, despite the fact that the display was a soft beach towel and a toothbrush holder! But I persevered and with the wonderful support of my friend, I experienced my best Christmas ever.

For three months I drove from store to store across Melbourne, having so much fun and getting paid for it! I had never realized before how much I enjoyed being creative! Amazingly, this temporary job turned into several years of casual work with that company, a new career direction and my completion of a full qualification in Visual Merchandising a few years later. To get me started, the rehabilitation service assisted by paying some of the training fees in order for me to complete that qualification.

Pearls (My Long Term Recovery Management)

I was astounded at how gently and beautifully the Lord had turned me toward another career and in a direction which continues to this day, opening up opportunities for me to be creative. I could never have predicted this change in the course of my life, nor that I would find such satisfaction and joy.

7.

Determination (Recovery and Today)

WE HAVE REACHED THE final chapter of my story and now I would like to tell you what life is like for me now, in my mid-50s. I'll remind you of my motivations for writing and tell you about the struggles and encouragements that were involved in spurring me on to write my story for you. I've included some analogies that are significant for me.

I like to use analogies because they remind me of how I related my faith to being sick and motivated myself to continue to be constructive and positive. Where does this preferred method of communication come from? It's just the way I think. Thinking styles are wonderfully diverse. My preferred thinking style is expressive, characterized by *"interpersonal, spiritual and emotional aspects. Together, these would express themselves in intuitive, insightful thinking, both in the feeling and problem-solving processes."*[1] (HBDI Herrmann Brain dominance instrument. Copyright Herrmann Global, 2009–2017. C quadrant 3211 page 25).

This is why I was drawn to nursing as my first career choice and why I enjoy roles that are people-related and organizational.

---

1. HBDI Herrmann Brain dominance instrument. Copyright Herrmann Global, 2009–2017. C quadrant 3211 page 25. Used with permission.

Determination (Recovery and Today)

During my acute illness, somehow I was able to keep intact my trust in the God revealed in Jesus Christ and made present in my life by the Spirit. I think this was because I am convinced that no experience, however negative, is ever outside of God's plan for our eventual good. What I know for sure is that God never gave up on me even in my darkest hours. He was alongside me all the way, holding my hand. I journaled these thoughts: "Now that I've survived this distressing experience, maybe God can use my story to help someone else." This became my principle motivation for this book. I wanted to destigmatize OCD in Christian circles. Christians have had a tough time for too long when they experience mental illnesses. There is so little material available to help Christians living under the awful burden of OCD and other anxiety disorders, and even less for their family or friends.

This fact may well be linked to the issues identified in the following excerpt from an article by psychiatrist Dr. Robert Yewers titled, 'Psychiatry and Christianity', again in *Luke's Journal*, 2002,

> . . . just as most Christians no longer regard physical illness as a punishment from God, neither should we say this of mental illness. Many Christians feel guilty when they experience psychiatric illness, thinking that they must be spiritually weak or deficient because they have developed depression or some other disorder. Frequently, depressed people view the world in a negative and pessimistic way. This flows directly from their depression, which affects thought as well as emotion. If at this time their faith is questioned, it can lead to a significant deterioration and a sense of abandonment by God. This is, in fact, related to their mental illness rather than a crisis of faith.[2]

In my earlier chapters I spoke about my feelings of guilt and deficiency. Perhaps by sharing my story, I could assist in enlightening Christians about my experience of the reality of mental illness and differentiate it from faith issues. Perhaps I could encourage any sufferers like me not to give up their hope of recovery and life

---

2. Yewers, "Psychiatry and Christianity." 8.

fulfilment. Perhaps my story could help reduce, a little, the distress of another Christian in a similar situation. Perhaps my story could help someone identify that the fears that are overwhelming them may be in fact obsessions and compulsions and they might therefore seek help earlier.

STARTING WITH A RECORD

Very early on in my illness I wanted to keep a record of my experience so that later, when things weren't so tough for me, I could look back to see God's amazing grace throughout it. I didn't want to forget the motivational quotes I'd read and heard, the songwriters' lyrics that I'd applied to my life or the encouragements of family and friends. I didn't want to forget the life lessons that God had revealed to me along the way! Truths like freedom from perfectionism, self-acceptance and the need for courage and perseverance in implementing my treatment strategies; and other truths like how completely compatible my faith walk was with these strategies. At times when I hadn't been able to rely on many of the thought processes of my mind, I could look back at this record and remember where I was headed and why.

After the first decade from diagnosis had passed, this is how I described my feelings about keeping a record in my journal,

"I need to look to the treasures given to me by God, doctors, friends and family over the last 10 or so years, relive them, activate them to spur me on and preserve them as living treasures for the future to draw upon." That's why I describe these treasures as precious pearls of wisdom, figuratively the glow worms' milky light that were glimmers of hope, helping to lead me out of that lava tube of anxiety and depression.

In starting this record, *it wasn't long before I began to hope that perhaps what I wrote might be of benefit to other people.* Indeed, if I hadn't kept my journals I couldn't have recorded those emotions and experiences and this book would not exist.

DETERMINATION (RECOVERY AND TODAY)

The gold pen

In 2003 a close friend, Lisa, gave me an early Christmas present. It was a golden notebook for me to fill with my literary 'treasures'. She knew that I liked to write poetry and we were close enough for me to share my lava tube poem with her. By giving me this notebook, she sought to encourage me to write more. Inside its cover she had glued a printout of an inspiring prophecy by Bill Yount, founder of Blowing the Shofar Ministry, that she had recently read on the Internet and thought might inspire me:

> *I saw Gold Pens falling out of Heaven onto the earth as though they were being thrown by the angels like javelins into the hands of unknown people. I saw these pens turning into spears and swords as they fell into these hands. As their fingers began to write; books, songs and poetry were becoming lethal weapons to war against the enemy!*
>
> *Psalm 144:1 was being activated throughout the earth! "Blessed be the Lord my strength, who teaches my hands to war and my fingers to fight!" . . . Is there a book in you? A song stirring in your heart? Poetry that keeps coming to the surface? Perhaps the Lord is calling you this hour to pick your pen up!*[3]

Five years later I committed to writing this book. On the day after my birthday I posted a letter to Dr F, telling him about my decision and asking for some help with preliminary research. A week after that a birthday present from Mark's parents arrived for me in the post. At that time, they did not know about my intention. I gasped with surprise when I took off the gift wrap to find a gold pen, engraved with my name!

---

3. Yount, Bill C., "I Saw Gold Pens Falling Out of Heaven onto the Earth" lines 4–9, lines 33–36. Used with permission.

My own gold pen!

SETBACKS AND STRUGGLES

That gold pen arrived seven years ago. I'm now just past my mid-50s. You may be wondering why seven years have passed before my book was completed. There are several reasons for this.

First, I needed to be well enough to undertake the project. I needed to be very careful not to put myself under too much pressure when researching the signs and symptoms of OCD and my experiences. To look back again at the period of major mental instability where I couldn't function properly was risky. I shared with my mentor that I was worried about needing to describe the signs and symptoms when I was sickest. To include them in my book, would I inadvertently 'wake the sleeping giant' of my OCD? She cautioned me with this advice:

Jesus' yoke is easy and his burden is light[4]. *Therefore, God knows what he's doing and would never intend for this project to have a detrimental effect on your health. Let him share the load with*

---

4. With reference to Matthew 11:28–30.

Determination (Recovery and Today)

you and take the bulk of the weight. Even though this is my story of healing and grace of God, it's also his story, so don't set a timeframe for its completion. It will be done in his timing.

Naturally, there were other times when being a mum and wife was a much higher priority than writing. I'm sure this is the same for most wives and parents! So, I would lay the book down for a season. I also needed carpal tunnel surgery and thanks to modern technology I was able to utilize voice-activated software for much of the writing of this book.

But other times it was just too hard in all respects to press on. During those times I kept Psalm 32:7-8 quietly within in my heart:

> You are my hiding place; you will protect me from trouble and surround me with songs of deliverance. I will instruct you and teach you in the way you should go; I will counsel you with my loving eye on you. Psalm 32:7-8 NIV

I laid down this project many times. When I would tentatively consider picking it up again my family and friends would encourage me. At those times I thought of the Apostle Paul's analogy in his letter to the Hebrews, of an enthusiastic spectator crowd watching the end stage of a marathon. Here's The Message version:

> Discipline in a Long-Distance Race. Do you see what this means—all these pioneers who blazed the way, all these veterans cheering us on? It means we'd better get on with it. Strip down, start running—and never quit! Hebrews 12:1 (The Message)

I could, symbolically, look up to the grandstand and see them leaning over the spectator fences, drumming their hands against the barriers, hollering encouragements and waving paper streamers for me to finish this marathon.

The radio broadcast

In September 2014, despite being nearly halfway through draft four, I decided that finishing this book was just too hard. So instead I decided to submit a very abridged five-minute version to the ABC, (774) Melbourne radio station for its 'Changing Tracks' segment. This segment is presented by journalist Rafael Epstein. Every Friday at 5 PM he plays a listener's song that was playing when that person's life 'changed tracks'. Before he plays the track, Rafael reads out the story that the listener has written about that turning point in their life. The stories might be happy or sad, momentous or sweetly simple.

I was so excited that my story was chosen to be read out at the end of National Mental Health Week October 2014, along with the song that was playing when my life 'changed tracks'. The song I chose to represent when my life changed track was *Permission to Shine*[5], written by American songwriter Bridget Benenate and performed by Australian Pop Duo Bachelor Girl. I loved this song because it is a song of hope and release from self-condemnation. In my story I included Patricia Deegan's quote that each of us carries within a precious flame, a spark of the divine[6] because it is so broadly relevant. A full transcript of the broadcast story is in Appendix 1.

FINISHING THE MARATHON

I listened to that live radio broadcast whilst sitting on my bed, with big, warm, salty tears trickling into my smiling mouth. Now my story had been broadcast across all of Melbourne and was stored on the Internet sound cloud. The mandate given to me to write this story was completed. Promptly, I packed up all my resources and all my reference books, stored my manuscript on a USB stick and put them in a crate under our house. I even threw out my text books of tips on how to publish a book.

---

5. Permission to Shine written by Benenate, Bridget Louise. Rights Management: Benenate, Universal Music Publishing MGB Australia and O-Connor Songs. Performed by Bachelor Girl (Tania Doko and James Roche), Album: "Waiting for the Day" 1999.

6. Deegan, "Recovering Our Sense of Value after Being Labelled Mentally Ill." 7–11. Used with permission.

Determination (Recovery and Today)

But God had other things in mind. A month later, a close friend, Kerryn, shared a beautiful truth she had recently learned which made me reconsider this project. She said:

If I don't give you the best of me then you miss out on what I have to offer and if you don't give me the best of you then I miss out on who you are and all that you have to offer. Being fully me encourages you to be fully you. I will understand you much more fully when you finish your book.

Around about this time I was referred back to Dr F for a review of my medication. I hadn't consulted him for nine years. He enquired after my book and mentioned that stories like these still need to be told. He elaborated that the average length of time that an undiagnosed person with OCD might take before they seek treatment is three years. Perhaps by making my story available in a book it might help reduce that timeframe and the need for medication in the short or long term or at all.

That weekend I enlisted Mark's help to bring the crate back upstairs. I dusted it off, notified Kevin, my patient reader and primary editor, and began working to finish the project.

TODAY

Now, sixteen years after my mind broke, I'll tell you how my mental health is these days. In a nutshell I've recovered. Under psychiatric advice, I remain on a modern anti-anxiety/depression medication permanently. I accept this as a fact of my life and am very grateful that this kind of modern medication is available to assist me.

I can identify those stresses that trigger my OCD, and take the initiative to manage these stressors and seek medical advice if needed. To help me gauge this, I ask myself a question which is characteristically Australian: "Are my daily worries becoming a bit 'dodgy'"? By this I mean, is OCD infiltrating my thought processes and influencing my behavior? The word 'dodgy' means unreliable, tricky and untrustworthy. I then gain reassurance from Proverbs 3 as I go to seek medical advice.

> Trust in the Lord with all your heart, and do not lean on your own understanding. In all your ways acknowledge him, and he will make straight your paths. Proverbs 3:5–6 NIV

Am I still bothered by obsessions and compulsions? Yes, from time to time. An example is from a position I worked in recently; I locked my work office and was heading home. I had walked for five minutes when I was interrupted by an intrusive thought that I hadn't locked my filing cabinet. I suddenly stopped in the middle of the footpath to think about this while all the other office workers continued to bustle around and passed me on their way home. "I should be like them, hurrying home from work and not standing in the middle of footpath thinking about my insignificant filing cabinet," I thought to myself. I could feel a summer breeze on my face as I vacillated between going back to check the filing cabinet or continuing to go home. This breeze seemed to tease me with its gentleness compared to the worried struggle inside my head. After a few more seconds' deliberation I doggedly decided to go on home.

Sometimes I struggle with where I park my car. I can't tolerate the tow ball hanging over a pedestrian footpath space by even a centimeter, lest someone bump into it, break their leg, hit their head and suffer a lifetime of permanent injury.

Sometimes I worry that if I leave my sunglasses on the passenger seat of my car they will start a fire by the same physics as scouts start a camp fire with a magnifying glass and sunshine! To take up the challenge of this thought, sometimes I'll deliberately leave my sunglasses in full sunshine inside my car, despite the worry that it causes me, knowing that my fears are ridiculous.

Sometimes I do give in to an obsessional thought and seek the reassurance of others' opinions thereby 'recruiting' them to help relieve my worry for me.

I saved this manuscript onto a USB that I carried in my handbag in case my house burned down and I lost all my treasures, my record and the pearls of wisdom that I've been given. Is that OCD or just a sensible precaution?

But despite the remnants of my OCD predisposing me to these fears, when I find something funny I laugh loud! This is because I know how dark life can get and now I can appreciate how beautiful my life is! By beauty I mean that even though I still live with OCD and it has shaped some of my life, it doesn't define me. I don't allow myself to recall the memories of those dark times beyond my descriptions of them in this book, because it's not constructive for me to do so. I do need to take it easy in how much I commit to and how much rest I get because I don't have limitless emotional energy. I'm a lover of Nanna naps to rest my mind and now that I am a grandmother, I feel validated!

Volunteering and employment

In respect to these, I moved on from retail work into administration. But I still missed the contact with the general public that nursing had brought me. In an attempt to fill this need, I volunteered at the 2006 Melbourne Commonwealth Games as a general public assistant. I never imagined that I would be the person sitting in a tennis umpire's chair announcing, through a loud hailer, the venue directions for thousands of cycling race spectators on the banks of the Yarra River. Nevertheless, that was me!

Five years later I still missed involvement with the general public, so I volunteered to help at the Mother's Day classic 5 km walk, around Melbourne's Royal Botanical Gardens. I stood in the rain with my fellow volunteers, handing out cups of water and saying "Well done, well done"! to hundreds and hundreds of walkers at the finish line. "I absolutely love this"! I prayed. That night I resolved to look for new employment where I could make a more direct contribution to people's lives. As nursing was out of the question, I was blessed to gain employment as a receptionist in a community refugee and asylum seeker support program, where I worked for several years.

I became one of that office's First-Aiders and completed a two-day Mental Health First Aid program. This program, founded in Australia in 2000 by Betty Kitchener OAM and Professor Tony

Jorm, has already spread to at least 21 countries. Thousands of people have now been through these courses. This indicates that our society now recognizes we need sound basic steps to assist someone who is developing a mental health problem or is in a mental health crisis.

I was also responsible for the Occupational Health & Safety inductions of new team members. You can imagine that for someone like me, this responsibility could be a mine field of anxiety, but I didn't let 'Gollum' get the better of me and I was able to carry out this role comfortably. I was also able to 'event manage' large meetings and events, knowing that my attention to detail (with a little OCD in the mix) was efficient enough that the organizational requirements are usually all covered!

Feedback from family and friends

In order to gain an independent perspective of what life is now like with me, and to bring some validation to the aims of my story, I recently asked my close family and friends to describe me now.

Mark said:

> Today, you are outwardly competent, organized and effective in a complex full-time work role. You cope well with demanding people, stressful situations, and constraints that would frustrate or overwhelm many people. No one you interact with at work, church or community would recognize any symptoms of your OCD.
>
> Behind the scenes, I know you work hard at keeping this balance and maintaining this high level of functioning. You need more rest and recovery time than others do, and you often choose to opt out of social situations to reduce your mental workload. Occasionally certain situations at home stretch you . . . too much and you tell me that you still carry significant anxiety . . . but you recover well from them.
>
> This points to three underlying strengths: your learned methods of dealing with what is going on in your head; your strength of character in persistently choosing

to rise above the mental illness; and the depth of your spiritual foundations that give you stability and courage. This is the real story of your journey with mental illness—that all three layers work together to restore your capacity to function normally in the face of many challenges. And you do it with a smile on your face! Thank you!

My family and friends reported that my experience had resulted in me becoming more optimistic about my position, able to "look upward, forward and outward" with humor and faith in the Lord and myself . . . They were glad that I stayed determined and persevered through my situation, accepting help from the psychologists and psychiatrists. The main thing they could see was that I had grown stronger and more resilient. They also detected my enjoyment of laughter, which they described as coming from a good place where I now see humor in situations and laugh despite my circumstances.

My son fed back that I now had much more insight into my diagnosis of OCD. I am sure he is right. What this means is that now I am able to free up emotional energy to find satisfaction in my work. Along with this I'm more open-minded and have more empathy. I am also more motivated to help others, just as I'd been helped. I've also found that my expression through art and writing has made me more relaxed. I can leave tasks incomplete and focus on what's important instead of obsessively striving to control my world.

My mentor used Jesus' metaphor of the vine and the branches, where Christians are advised to stay close to him so that we can flourish. She said that I'd responded well to hard pruning and become well established in his big vine. Whether I succeed or fail in what I do, God is still achieving his goals through me.

> "I am the true vine, and my Father is the gardener. He cuts off every branch in me that bears no fruit, while every branch that does bear fruit he prunes so that it will be even more fruitful. You are already clean because of the word I have spoken to you. Remain in me, as I also remain in you. No branch can bear fruit by itself; it must remain in the vine. Neither can you bear fruit unless you

remain in me. "I am the vine; you are the branches. If you remain in me and I in you, you will bear much fruit; apart from me you can do nothing. John 15:1–5 NIV

Lisa, who gave me the golden notebook all those years ago, gave me this feedback:

You are now more at peace, enjoying the creativity that is a natural well from within. It bubbles out of you like a babbling brook on a sunny day. The storm and torrential rain of OCD no longer drowns out the brook's joyful sound or drowns out the senses.

MY CONTINUING HOPES: THE STORY OF DAVID AND GOLIATH.

We have nearly reached the end of my story. If you have OCD or suspect that you might, I want to reiterate my continuing hopes for you. Please remember that it is a recognized and treatable illness with many effective strategies that can be enlisted to help you recover. You may feel completely ill-equipped to stand up to OCD or daunted at the prospect of starting. Therefore, I'd like to use a little of the story of David and Goliath to illustrate how you might like to start.

The story of David and Goliath comes from the Old Testament Book First Samuel chapter 17. Briefly it's the true story of a teenage shepherd named David, who grew up to become the most famous and respected king of Israel. His nation Israel was at war with the Philistines. Because David was young and the eighth son of his family, he couldn't join his brothers in the army. Instead he had to take responsibility for his father's flock of sheep.

One day David was sent down to the Israel army base to give his brothers some food supplies. The Philistines were proud of their fiercest warrior, Goliath, a huge man, at least 2 meters tall. He verbally taunted the Israelite army on a daily basis. All the Israelite troops, including their king Saul, were intimidated by him and didn't know what to do. Once David reached the army base he

Determination (Recovery and Today)

heard for himself the dreaded Goliath, goading the Israelite army. He accepted Goliath's challenge to single combat, and ended up killing Goliath before the giant had even reached him. David ran toward him and sling-shot the first of five smooth stones that he had earlier put in his knapsack, into Goliath's forehead.

David was not, as children's books sometimes illustrate, a small boy with no skills except bravado guarding fluffy white sheep in a tranquil green paddock. Even though he was a youth, he had years of experience caring for and protecting his father's flock overnight in the wild. He wanted his father to be proud of how well he looked after them. After all, that flock of sheep was an important commodity to the family. He'd trained and refined his defensive and offensive skills with at least two war weapons, the slingshot and the club so well that he'd even kill a lion *and* a bear to protect them. His slingshot was a serious weapon. He knew he always needed to be prepared for the unexpected. So he always kept his shepherd's kid skin knapsack with him, filled with food, supplies, his slingshot and five stones.

How might this story relate to beginning to manage OCD?

- OCD is a bully like Goliath (and Gollum)
- OCD is an illness of pathological doubt. These doubts are a little like Goliath's intimidation which wore down the Israelite army's confidence, until they and he thought he was invincible. In fact, he wasn't. OCD's obsessive thoughts, images or impulses are intrusive and inappropriate and cause a great deal of distress.
- OCD is not worth negotiating with, just like the arrogant Goliath.
- OCD takes courage to stand up to, just like David needed.
- Some aspects of CBT management of OCD may seem counterintuitive like David, without any armor, taking the offensive up to Goliath with just a sling shot weapon.
- David's knapsack held not only his secret weapons—the five smooth stones—but also essential supplies. OCD requires us to learn and use a variety of management strategies.

In making a start in managing OCD, what 'supplies' might you take in your own 'knapsack'? Perhaps you would join a support group, have the phone number of a helpline handy, or have the next appointment date with your counsellor entered in your smart phone.

Importantly, remember, in taking steps to learn to manage OCD, you haven't yet developed the skills that David honed whilst tending his father's flock. So it's okay to start your offensive using pebbles instead of slingshot stones. Pebbles may be small but they can still hurt, especially when they hit a shin bone!

If you are already on your own journey of management, I hope my story will help you to continue to throw bigger and bigger stones at Goliath (or in my case Gollum), until you are in charge, not him. Even though boy David only packed five, you can use stockpiles of them! There isn't a limit!

I pray that you'll always hope and be gentle with yourself.

> God is our refuge and strength, an ever-present help in trouble. Psalm 46:1 NIV

In closing, I'd like to share with you my final and most precious story of all.

Four months before my mind broke, Mark and I celebrated our sixteenth wedding anniversary with a weekend on the South Gippsland coast. We stayed the night in a cozy bed-and-breakfast. That evening had been hot and stifling but a squally cool change swept through the region in the early hours of the morning, dropping the temperature and cleansing the air.

After breakfast we took a morning walk along a quiet beach at Powlett Creek. As we enjoyed the refreshing light drizzle in that wild place, we spotted what at first looked like a pinecone on the beach. It was in fact, a bedraggled young ringtail possum stranded below the scrubby bank.

How did it get there? Being nocturnal, perhaps it had become disorientated in the evening storm or been blown out of a gum tree. It was too weak to scale the one meter bank to the safety and familiar territory of the bush. We realized it would not survive in

Determination (Recovery and Today)

this exposed place for much longer. At any moment a feral cat or bird of prey might easily catch it.

Mark bent down to pick it up, intending to lift it up the bank. As he did so the little possum did a very sad thing. Instead of putting up a fight for self-preservation with its teeth and claws, it closed its wide, terrified eyes in complete surrender to inevitable death at the hands of the big human predator looming over it.

Mark lifted it up in both hands and gently set it down on the bank. It lurched off towards the shelter of the coastal scrub and was last seen disappearing into the safety of the undergrowth.

My daughter's interpretation of the Little Possum Story (2015)

In the early months after my diagnosis, I compared myself to that young possum, full of dread and very lost. But just as Mark had saved its life, the hands that saved me were God's.

> In a desert land he found him, in a barren and howling waste. He shielded him and cared for him; he guarded him as the apple of his eye. Deuteronomy 32:10 NIV

Appendix

Changing Tracks Broadcast, 10th October 2014[1]

Changing tracks with Rafael Epstein

"EVERYTHING WAS OBSESSIVELY DOUBTED, AND THE LIFE WAS ALL BUT SQUEEZED OUT OF ME."

THIS WOULD BE A different story if I had tripped and broken my leg.

If you break your leg, you usually get to choose the color of your plaster cast and you get flowers and casseroles.

But no, my story is about how I broke my mind as I walked back from our compost bin, twenty meters from the back door.

I didn't trip over anything, but something broke in me all the same.

It was May 26th, 2001.

I 'broke' when I was 40 years old, a wife of sixteen years and a mum of two small children.

A trained nurse of 20 years' experience, and a committed Christian, I thought these long months of anxiety must be some kind of spiritual challenge.

---

1. Epstein, Rafael. "Rosemary-Changing Tracks "Everything was obsessively doubted, and the life was all but squeezed out of me." Full document. Printed with permission.

Appendix

I thought reducing my commitments would solve the problem.

Then one day at the school where I worked, a girl was brought to my sick bay.

After a twenty-minute rest she felt better.

I wrote a note for her mum but later in the day I suddenly I felt a "click" in my mind and thought "Oh no! Did I miss something? It could be too late to save her!"

Then the sensible Rosemary took over.

"Don't be silly," I thought, "you know she's fine. There's no need to worry".

The following weekend, away with family, I knew I would not enjoy.

Questions kept flying around in my head in ever anxiety-raising intensity.

Had I correctly assessed her? How was she now? How could I ever forgive myself if she becomes seriously ill or even died?

I decided to take my portable radio with me.

I'd sneak off and listen to it in our room to hear if there had been an outbreak of illness in a school girl.

A few days later, another school girl received a little nip on her finger from the school rabbit.

It was a tiny bite that didn't even break the skin.

But not in my OCD world. Her mother needs to know in case the little girl dies.

I wrote a note for her to take home.

What if she loses the note? What if her mum doesn't realize the risks?

I rang her home and left a message with her grandmother.

But I had my doubts. What if Grandma didn't tell the mum?

So I rang again.

This time Grandma was a little terse.

I knew what I'd done was really stupid and I felt such a dill. At this stage my coping mechanisms were failing badly.

I couldn't stop the pathological questioner I later called "Gollum".

He needled me with ridiculously implausible thoughts, my actions would have disastrous consequences.

I was terrified. I couldn't shut him up.

Everything was obsessively doubted, and the life was all but squeezed out of me.

On that day, walking from the compost bin in our backyard, I ran out of any emotional reserves.

I thought to myself, "this can't be happening! This is what other people do when they can't cope. This is not me".

I walked away from my doctor with a starter pack of anti-anxiety pills, a blood test to be done and a psychiatric referral.

A few weeks? later I was diagnosed with Obsessive Compulsive Disorder and Major Depression.

I felt humiliated. I was convinced I'd let my family down and it's entirely my fault.

It was not until months later that I accepted that all this was not my fault at all.

My feelings were a result of a mental illness that had slowly taken over my life.

I was comforted by the words from Patricia Deegan.

> You may have been diagnosed with a mental illness, but you are not an illness. You are a human being whose life is precious and is of infinite value. You are precious and good. You are not insane. You do not belong in institutions for the rest of your life. You don't belong on the streets. You are a human being. You carry within you a precious flame, a spark of the divine. You were born to love and to be loved. That's your birthright. Mental illness cannot take that from you. Nobody can take that from you.[2]

I became more skilled at managing the OCD.

I began to bask in the bliss of relief.

Instead of tensely curling up, and with pathological fears dissolving, I could enjoy lovely, sweet relief!

---

2. Deegan, "Recovering Our Sense of Value after Being Labelled Mentally Ill." 7–11.

APPENDIX

It's thirteen years now since I broke my mind, a long journey along a convoluted path to understanding, relief, acceptance and liberty.

Do I still have OCD? Yes.

Do I still take medication? Yes.

Does this disappoint me? Somewhat, but it doesn't vex me.

It's an example of implementing my strategy to recognize a change in my condition and be proactive about it.

Now when I laugh, I laugh loud!

But I am not a limitless ball of sanguine energy.

I frequently need "down time" and have to watch out for that diabolical Gollum undermining my health.

I regularly need to remind myself of several foundations of emotional health that I have battled to lay like self-acceptance, perseverance and tenacity.

I recalled hearing my young daughter singing along to this song on our car radio in the months after my breakdown.

It was, in a nut shell, a song about easing up on the self-condemnation, and giving myself, permission to shine.[3]

Even though my life jumped tracks onto a dark route that I never booked a ticket for, nevertheless, with the help of family, friends and medical professionals, I learned to shine.

So, this week's Changing Track is for Rosemary.

---

3. Permission to Shine written by Benenate, Bridget Louise. Rights Management: Benenate, Universal Music Publishing MGB Australia and O-Connor Songs. Performed by Bachelor Girl (Tania Doko and James Roche), Album: "Waiting for the Day" 1999.

Bibliography

Anxiety Recovery Centre Victoria. "Obsessive Compulsive Disorder OCD." http://arcvic.com.au/anxiety-disorders/obsessive-compulsive-disorder
Anxiety Recovery Centre Victoria. "What is Recovery?" http://www.arcvic.org.au/recovery/whatisrecovery
Anxiety Recovery Centre Victoria. "CBT and Behavioural Therapy." http://www.arcvic.com.au/obsessive-compulsive-disorder/19
Better Health Channel, "Obsessive Compulsive Disorder—Family and Friends." https://www.betterhealth.vic.gov.au/health/conditionsandtreatments/obsessive-compulsive-disorder-family-and-friends
Bloch, Sidney. *Understanding Troubled Minds*. Carlton: Melbourne University Press, 2011.
Deegan, Patricia. "Recovering Our Sense of Value after Being Labelled Mentally Ill." *Journal of Psychological Nursing*, Vol 31 No 4 (1993) 7–11.
Delbridge, A., Bernard, J.R.L., Blair, D., Butler, P. and Yallop, C, eds. *The Macquarie Dictionary Revised Third Edition*, Sydney: Macquarie University, 1997.
Dunjey, Lachlan. "Depression and the Christian." *Luke's Journal of Christian Medicine and Dentistry* Volume 7 No.3 (2002) 10–11.
Forty, Sandra. *M.C.Escher*. Surrey: TAJ INTERNATIONAL, 2009
l'Anson, Kathryn. . . . *Nine, Ten, Do It Again: A Guide to Obsessive Compulsive Disorder for People with OCD and Their Families*. © Kathryn l'Anson-Dandenong: SmithKline Beecham, Obsessive Compulsive & Anxiety Disorders Foundation of Victoria Inc.
l'Anson, Kathryn and Carne, Rod, *A Guide for Young People with Obsessive Compulsive Disorder*. Ashwood: Anxiety Recovery Centre Victoria, 2005.
Krauth, Laurie. "Scrupulosity: Blackmailed by OCD in the Name of God." http://lauriekrauth.weebly.com/scrupulosity-blackmailed-by-ocd-in-the-

Bibliography

name-of-god.html *OCF Newsletter* Spring 2007. *Anxiety Matters* Vol 12, No 3 May (2008) 4,5,9

McGrath, Patrick B. *The OCD Answerbook: Professional Answers to More than 250 Top Questions about Obsessive-Compulsive Disorder.* Naperville: Sourcebooks, 2007.

Nelson, J.S. Abramowitz, S.P. Whiteside & B.J. Deacon, "Scrupulosity in patients with obsessive–compulsive disorder: Relationship to clinical and cognitive phenomena" *Journal of Anxiety Disorders* (2006) 20, 1071–1086.

Parks Victoria, "Mount Eccles National Park—Visitor Guide and Walks." *Park Notes* March (2001) 1–4.

Schwartz, Jeffrey M. with Beyette, Beverly. *Brain Lock: Free Yourself from Obsessive-Compulsive Behaviour.* New York: Regan, 1996.

Stokes, Jess. "Law and Disorder." *Warcry* Volume 121 No.7 (2002) 6–7.

Thomas, Lauren. "Anxiety and Depression" *Cultivate Training Session, Youth for Christ* 18/11/2009.

Yewers, Robert. "Psychiatry and Christianity". *Luke's Journal of Christian Medicine and Dentistry* Volume 7 No.3 (2002) 8–9.

Yount, Bill C., "I Saw Gold Pens Falling Out of Heaven onto the Earth." http://www.elijahlist.com/words/display_word.html?ID=1783.

www.ingramcontent.com/pod-product-compliance
Lightning Source LLC
Chambersburg PA
CBHW070919180426
43192CB00038B/1965